Monika Kratz

# TOR GUNDERSEN
## WERKE · WORKS · 作品集

Photography:
Svein-Erik Tøraasen

STICHTING KUNSTBOEK

Monika Kratz

# TOR GUNDERSEN
## WERKE · WORKS · 作品集

Photography:
Svein-Erik Tøraasen

STICHTING KUNSTBOEK

# VORWORT

Wie kommt eine deutsche Journalistin auf die Idee ein Buch über einen norwegischen Floristen zu schreiben? Die Antwort ist einfach: Sie ist vom Fach, begeistert sich für seine schönen, oft minimalistischen Floralobjekte und zählt diese zum Interessantesten, was die Floristen weltweit zu bieten haben. Das allein wäre Grund genug einen Bildband mit Arbeiten von Tor Gundersen herauszubringen. Aber es gibt noch eine weitere Komponente: die persönliche Begegnung. Sie ermöglichte einen spannenden Einblick in das Wirken eines ungewöhnlichen Menschen. Ungewöhnlich, weil ehrlich und einfach, und darin so konsequent, dass eine verblüffend harmonische Einheit zwischen Person und Werk existiert.

Dies anhand einiger charakteristischer „Momentaufnahmen" zu skizzieren, die Ihnen den Floraldesigner und seine Floristik näherbringen sollen, ist der Sinn und Zweck des Porträtteils. Erlauben Sie mir, neben dem Bestreben nach fachlicher Objektivität auch meine respektvolle Verbundenheit zu offenbaren - wenn auch nur zwischen den Zeilen. Es könnte leicht ein Vielfaches geschrieben werden, Stoff gibt es genug. Doch schließlich soll noch Raum für Fantasie bleiben. Der Bildteil in diesem Buch mit den neuesten, wunderbar gestalteten und großartig fotografierten Arbeiten von Tor Gundersen hat ohnehin seine eigene Sprache.

*Monika Kratz*

Kerpen, im Oktober 2001

# PREFACE

How does a German journalist arrive at the idea of writing a book about a Norwegian florist? The answer is very simple: she is a florist herself, has a great personal interest in his often minimalist floral creations and considers them to be among the most fascinating achievements of any florist worldwide. Reason enough to publish a picture book on the works of Tor Gundersen. But there is also another factor involved: the personal contact. Meeting him personally and working with him have provided an exciting insight into the life and work of this extraordinary person. Extraordinary in that he is honest and uncomplicated in every aspect of his life, something that has created an amazingly harmonious unit – encompassing his work and his person.

The portrait section of the book illuminates this with a few characteristic "candid shots", intended to bring you closer to the floral designer and his floristry. As I strive to maintain a certain level of professional objectivity, allow me, if you will, to lend expression to my great respect and admiration for Tor Gundersen – even if only between the lines.

Volumes could have been written; there is certainly enough to be said. But it is also important to leave some things to the imagination. After all, the photo section of the book, with fantastic photos illustrating the latest wonderful creations of Tor Gundersen, also speaks a language of its own.

*Monika Kratz*

Kerpen, in October 2001

# 序文

ドイツ人ジャーナリストがノルウェー人フローリストの本を作るというアイディアがどうして浮かんだのでしょうか？その答えはとてもシンプルです。筆者は専門家であり、フローリストの耽美的かつ、時にミニマムなオブジェに感激し、またその美しさは世界中のフロリスティックに従事する人々に紹介するに値するとみなしたからです。それだけでトゥルー・グンダーセンの作品集を出版するに十分な理由ですが、もう一つの理由は個人的な出会いでした。筆者は彼から非凡な印象を受けたのです。非凡、それは誠実で、シンプル、そしてその人柄と作品には驚くほど調和の取れた一貫性が存在するからです。

読者の方々にそのフラワーデザイナーと彼のフロリスティックを親しんでもらえる、いくつかの個性ある"スナップ写真"の概要をポートレート部に載せています。

専門的な客観性志向もさることながら、私たちの信頼関係を行間から読み取って頂けるならばありがたいです。

資料がいくらでもあるならば、もっとたくさんの事が書けたでしょうが、最後には想像を書き立てる空間も残していなければならないのです。整然と構成、撮影されたトゥルー・グンダーセンの最新作は言うまでもなく、彼自身の言葉なのです。

*Monika Kratz*

モニカ・クラッツ
ケアーペン，2001年10月

# INHALT · CONTENTS · 目次

WERKE · WORKS · 作品

ANHANG · APPENDIX · 付録

# PORTRÄT
# PORTRAIT
# ポートレート

VORGESTELLT: TOR GUNDERSEN

SKIZZIERTE MOMENTE EINES FLORISTENLEBENS


PROFILE: TOR GUNDERSEN

SKETCHED MOMENTS IN THE LIFE OF A FLORIST


プロフィール: トゥルー・グンダーセン

フローリスト人生

# NATUR

Im „Fjell" entdeckt: *Dryas octopetala*,
die Weiße Silberwurz (1997)

Discovery in the "fjell": *Dryas octopetala*,
mountain avens (1997)

"フィエル"での発見: バラ科-octopetala (1997)

Ruhepol „Zuhause": die westnorwegische
Küste bei Ulsteinvik (1997)

Oasis "at home": West Norwegian coast near
Ulsteinvik (1997)

落ち着く所"故郷": 西ノルウェー・ウルシュタイン
ヴィック近郊の海岸 (1997)

### Freiheitsliebend & heimatverbunden

Es ist eine Eigenheit der Norweger, heißt es, jede Gelegenheit zu nutzen hinauszugehen in die Berge und Wälder. Sie verbringen freie Tage und Ferien auf ihrer „hytte" (Wochenendhäuschen), ohne Luxus, idealerweise außer Sichtweite aller anderen, rundum Natur pur. Das heißt atmen können, den Hauch der Freiheit spüren. Sie lieben ihre Heimat sehr. Auch die Städter bewahren diese ausgeprägte Naturverbundenheit. Die dramatischste und deshalb faszinierendste Region (manche sagen von ganz Europa) ist Westnorwegen mit seiner wildzerklüfteten Fjordlandschaft. Dort ist Tor Gundersen aufgewachsen. Die Eltern führten die Kinder von klein auf an die schönsten Plätze, zeigten ihnen Pflanzen und andere Dinge in der Natur, die sie für traditionelle häusliche Dekorationen sammelten. Mit Dankbarkeit erinnert sich Tor an diese anfänglichen Erlebnisse, die ihn prägten. Doch gab es etwas, das ihn von anderen unterschied: offenbar eine Art hochempfindlicher Sensoren, die ihm in die Wiege gelegt worden waren und ihn größte Freude und Befriedigung

über die unendliche Vielfalt und Schönheit der Natur empfinden ließen. Vor diesem Hintergrund mag man erahnen, mit welcher Intensität ein Mensch wie Tor Gundersen heute mit Natur umgeht. Das kindliche Spiel ist gestalterischer Absicht gewichen. Natur ist Inspiration für Neues. So ist es nicht „Natur", die der Betrachter in Tors Objekten entdeckt, sondern die Liebe zur Natur, der Stolz auf die Schätze der Heimat und die Freiheit der Entfaltung, die auch der unscheinbarsten Blume zuteil wird.

*„Begegnet man in Norwegen einem Troll, darf man ihn nicht beim Namen nennen, sonst erstarrt er zu Stein.*
*Geht es aber um die wichtigsten Floralgestalter unserer Zeit, muss man einen Namen laut sagen: Tor Gundersen. Ich freue mich über seinen Erfolg. Er hat ihn verdient!"*

Thea Kornherr (Deutschland), junge Floristin und Assistentin bei Demonstrationen

# NATURE

### Love of freedom & homeland

It is said of Norwegians that they take every possible opportunity to go to the mountains and forests of their beautiful country. Every day off or holiday is spent in the "hytte" (weekend cabin) usually without any luxuries, ideally hidden from view in an isolated spot and surrounded by nature in its purest form. There they can breathe and feel a sense of freedom. Norwegians love their country very much. Even the cities maintain this distinctive closeness to nature. The most dramatic and therefore most fascinating region (some say of all of Europe) is Western Norway with its wild and rugged mountains and fjords. It is here that Tor Gundersen grew up. From a very early age his parents took the children to the most beautiful places and showed them plants and other things in nature, which they also collected for traditional decorations for their home. Tor has fond memories of these early experiences, which left a lasting impression on him. But there was something about him that set him apart from others: it was as if he had been born with "high fidelity" sensors that made him able to enjoy and appreciate the infinite diversity and beauty of nature. With this in mind, one can begin to guess at how intensely a person like Tor Gundersen feels about nature as an adult. What was once child's play has now grown into artistic creativity. Nature is his inspiration for new experiments. Thus it is not "nature" that the observer discovers in Tor's creations, but rather his deep and abiding love for nature, his pride in the treasures of his homeland and the freedom of creating – reflected in even the tiniest flower.

*"If you meet up with a troll in Norway you should never call him by his name, or else he will turn to stone. But when talking about the most important floral designer of our time, you should shout his name out loud: Tor Gundersen. I am very happy about his success. He has certainly earned it!"*

Thea Kornherr (Germany), junior florist and assistant at demonstrations

# 自然

### 自由を愛する & 故郷と結ばれた

山や森に出かける機会を利用する事はノルウェー人の特徴と言えます。彼らは休日や休暇を"hytteヒュッテ"(週末を過ごす小さな家)で過ごします。贅沢なものはなに一つなく、ただ見渡す限りの自然。つまり自由を満喫できるのです。彼らは故郷をとても愛しています。都会に住む人々もこの自然との結びつきを保ち続けています。自然に裂けたフィヨルドの景観を備えた西ノルウェー地方はドラマチックで、それだからこそ魅了的な地域(ヨーロッパ人の多くが口にしています)です。彼の両親は子供達を幼い頃から美しい場所へと連れ出し、植物や自然に存在する物を示し、伝統的、家庭的なデコレーションのためにそれらを収集したのです。トゥルーは今日、彼を特徴付けるその幼い時期の経験に感謝しながらそれを思い出します。他人とは異なったもの、非常に敏感なセンサーを彼は持っているのです。そのセンサーはどうやら彼に生まれついたもので、限りない自然の多様性と美しさに大きな喜びと満足感を彼は感じるのです。ここからおぼろげに解るでしょう。トゥルー・グンダーセンのように感情豊かな人物が今日どのように自然と接しているのかを。幼児期の遊戯が創造性に強く影響したのです。自然は新しい物へのインスピレーションです。トゥルーの作品に見られるのは"自然"ではなく、自然への愛、故郷の宝物に対する誇り、目立たない花をも加える自由な発想です。

「ノルウェーでトロールに出会ったら、名前を付けてはなりません。石になってしまうのです。しかし、私たちの時代のフラワーデザイナーに関しては大きな声で名前を言わなければ。トゥルー・グンダーセン。彼の成功を楽しみにしています。彼は成功するに相応しいのです！」

テェア・コーンヘアー(ドイツ):フローリスト、デモンストレーションのアシスタント

# IDEE

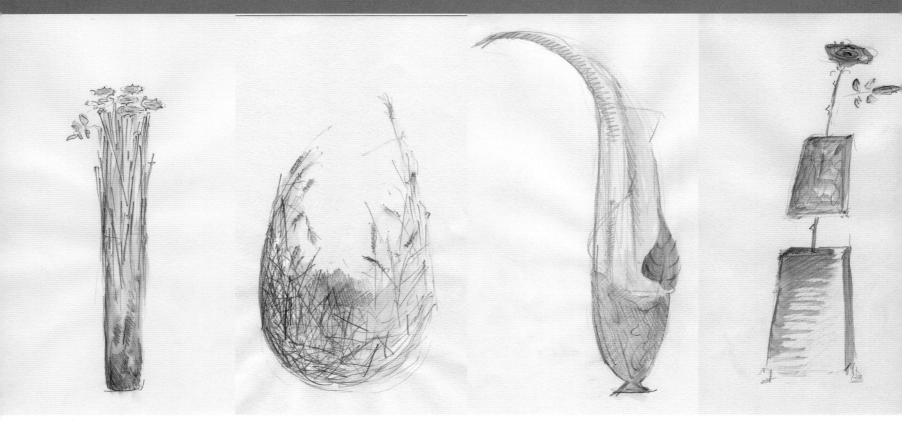

### Konzeptionell & minimalistisch

Das Zauberwort heißt Reduktion. Es trifft sehr gut die gestalterische Vorgehensweise von Tor Gundersen im Allgemeinen und gilt auch für die Werkstücke in diesem Buch. Der Begriff wird nur allzu oft für Gestaltungen mit wenig Blumen verwendet. Reduktion kann sich zwar auf die Menge beziehen, aber auch auf andere gestalterische Aspekte. Denn das Konzept bestimmt, was beschränkt werden soll: Farben oder Formen, Blumensorten oder Blütengrößen oder eine Kombination aus mehreren Aspekten. Reduktion bedeutet, dass alles Überflüssige, das, was der Umsetzung einer Idee nicht zuträglich ist, weil es keine Bedeutung und keinen Zusammenhang hat, weggelassen wird. Umso klarer wird die gestalterische Aussage „Reduzieren auf das Wesentliche". Das Prinzip scheint einfach zu sein. Dennoch ist das Weglassen das Schwierigste. Tor Gundersen ist darin ein Meister. Auf der Suche nach der perfekten Harmonie arbeitet er unermüdlich auch an den begleitenden Herausforderungen wie Schwerkraft, Proportion und Balance. Leichtigkeit im Ausdruck ist das Ziel. Die wichtigsten Themen, die sich bis heute herauskristallisiert haben, sind in diesem Buch als Kapitel zusammengefasst. „Die Gefäßform fortsetzen" – wer wäre darin so spezialisiert wie Tor Gundersen! Feinst aufeinander abgestimmte Farbnuancen, Strukturen und Umrisslinien lassen manchmal sogar den Übergang zwischen Gefäß und Floralem verschwinden. „Alte Formen neu entdeckt" bezieht sich auf Tors Anliegen, die vielen klassischen Formen aufzugreifen, nicht nur aus der Floristik, sondern aus allen gestalterischen Sparten, vom Kunsthandwerk bis zur Architektur: Pyramide und Kegel, Kugel und Ei, Urne und Vase, Säule und Kranz usw. Durch seine florale Umsetzung verleiht er diesen bereits existierenden Formen einen neuen Ausdruck. „West trifft Ost" stellt eine Symbiose von Elementen westlicher Floristik und den Einflüssen asiatischer Kunst und Kultur dar, die Tor auf seinen vielen Reisen nach Asien gesammelt hat. „Inspiration Norwegen" ist eine Hommage an sein Heimatland. Die verwendeten Pflanzen haben alle eine besondere Bedeutung, die durch die Art der Gestaltung auch für Nichtnorweger zu erahnen sind. Eben unverwechselbar Tor Gundersen!

# IDEA

## Conceptional & minimalist

The magic word here is reduction. Reduction describes the creative processes of Tor Gundersen very precisely and also applies to the floral arrangements in this book. It is a term that is used all too frequently when describing creations with few botanicals. But although reduction can refer to the number of flowers used, it can apply to other creative aspects of floristry. Because the basic concept determines what should be kept to a minimum: the colours or shapes, how many kinds of flowers or their sizes or a combination of these aspects. Reduction means that every element that is not essential to the implementation of the idea, either because it has no significance or connection, is to be left out. Which lends clarity to the creative statement "bare essentials". The principle appears quite simple. However, deciding which elements to leave out is not as easy as it might seem. Tor Gundersen is a master of reduction. In his quest for perfect harmony, he also experiments untiringly with related challenges, such as the force of gravity, proportion and balance. Expressing lightness is his main goal. The most important themes that have crystallized to date are compiled into the separate chapters of the book. "Continuation of Containers" – who could be more of a specialist at this than Tor Gundersen? Closely matched colour nuances, structures and outlines can sometimes make even the dividing line between a vase and its floral elements disappear. "Rediscovering existing Forms" refers to Tor's desire to use all kinds of existing classical forms, not only in floristry but also in all kinds of design-related works, from handicrafts to architecture, such as pyramids and cones, balls and egg shapes, urns and vases, columns and wreaths, etc. It is important for him not to lose those forms, but rather to give new looks to already existing forms. "West meets East" represents a symbiosis of elements of Western floristry and the influences of Asiatic art and culture that Tor has encountered on his many trips to Asia. And "Norwegian Inspiration" is a homage to his native land. All the plants used have a special significance that can even be understood by non-Norwegians, thanks to the creative way they are put together. Unmistakably Tor Gundersen!

# アイディア

## コンセプトのある & ミニマムな

この呪文は削減を意味しています。一般的にトゥルー・グンダーセンの創作方法はその的を獲ていて、この作品集に収められている作品もそうであると言えるでしょう。その概念は僅かな花材を用いたデザインによく役立てられています。削減とは分量だけではなく、その他すべてのデザインの観点にも関連しています。そして制限されるべきものがそのコンセプトとなるのです。色あるいは形、花の品種、花の大きさ、多様な視点からの組み合わせ。削減とはアイディアの転換に役立たないすべての余分なものです。それは省かれることに何の意味も、何の関連もないからです。こうして"本質を示す"という表現がより明らかになります。この原則は容易なようですが、省くということは最も難しいことです。トゥルー・グンダーセンはその点に関してマイスターと言えるでしょう。彼は完璧な調和を探しつつ、飽きることなく重心、プロポーション、バランスと言った付随物にも挑戦し、優しさを表現することを重視しています。今日までに現れた重要なテーマはこの作品集の各章に要約されています。"器の継続"-トゥルー・グンダーセンほどのスペシャリストがいるでしょうか！互いに相応しい上品な色のニュアンス、構成、輪郭線は時に花器と花材の変わり目をも隠してしまいます。"フォームの再発見"とはたくさんのクラッシックなフォームを取り入れるトゥルーの興味に関係しています。彼はフロリスティックだけではなく、芸術作品から建築に至るまでのすべての造形分野にまで関心を示しています。ピラミッドと円錐、球と楕円、壷と花瓶、円柱とリースなど。彼はこれらのすでに存在する型を花に転換し、新たに表現するのです。"西と東の出会い"は西洋のフロリスティックの要素と多くのアジア旅行の際に収集したその芸術と文化からの影響との共生を表現しています。"ノルウェーのインスピレーション"では彼の故郷への忠誠が表現されています。使用されている花材はすべて特別な意味を含み、その特別な意味はデザインを目にすればノルウェー人ではない人々にもおぼろげにわかる事でしょう。それこそ紛れもないトゥルー・グンダーセンです！

# MATERIALSUCHE

Abenteuer in Nesbru: der Seerosenteich (2000)

Adventure in Nesbru: water lily pond (2000)

ネスブリューでの冒険: 睡蓮の池 (2000)

Die ersten im Jahr: Leberblümchen, *Hepatica nobilis* (Bygdøy, Oslofjord, 1998)

The first of the year: liverwort, *Hepatica nobilis* (Bygdøy, Oslofjord, 1998)

一年中で一番早く咲く花: スハマソウ属-nobilis
(ビュグドゥイ、オスロフィヨルド、1998)

### Beharrlich & leidenschaftlich

Wo immer am Straßenrand etwas Blaues leuchtet und nicht auf Anhieb identifiziert werden kann, quietschen die Bremsen. Das muss einfach untersucht werden! Schließlich könnte es eine bis dahin unbekannte Blumenart sein, Grundlage für die nächste Kreation. Ein für ungeübte Augen langweilig-grün bewachsener Wall an der Autobahn - mühelos erkennt der Meister des floristischen Materials hier den dichten Bestand an Huflattich-Blättern. Findet irgendeinen Weg, das Halteverbot zu umgehen. Das ist die Chance! So viele auf einmal! Und weiß selbstverständlich auch schon, wie er die Ausbeute von fünf vollen Müllsäcken für eine Ladendekoration einsetzen wird. Die „Felsenkönigin", ein prächtiges Steinbrechgewächs, ist auch in schwindelnder Höhe nicht sicher vor den hartnäckigen Versuchen des in die Wand kletternden Tor Gundersen - barfuß, wenn gerade keine Wanderschuhe zur Hand sind. Goldrute in rauhen Mengen, *Filipendula ulmaria*, das Mädesüß, auch Leberblümchen, die ersten im Jahr – er weiß, wo sie zu finden sind. Kein Wunder, nach zwanzig Jahren Erfahrung kennt er Stellen im ganzen Land. Nie endet eine Fahrt mit leeren Händen. Und dann war da noch der Seerosenteich in der Nähe von Oslo. Den hat er zufällig im Frühjahr entdeckt und als im Sommer die Idee für ein Wasser-Objekt gereift ist, kauft er ein aufblasbares Gummiboot, rudert auf den Teich und erntet Blüten und Blätter. Blutegel und sonstiges Zubehör kümmern nicht. Einen Tag später drücken sich die Passanten am Schaufenster in Oslo die Nase platt...

# MATERIAL FORAYS

### Persevering & passionate

Whenever there is a bright flash of blue that cannot be immediately identified along the side of the road, the squeal of brakes will inevitably be heard. The matter simply must be investigated! After all, it could be the discovery of a previously unknown species of plant that could form the basis for his next creation. What appears to the untrained eye as merely a wall covered in some boring greens beside the highway will be effortlessly recognized by the master of floristic materials as a shaggy patch of coltsfoot. No time to worry about the 'no stopping' ordinance now. This is the chance of a lifetime – so much of it growing in one place! And naturally he already knows how he is going to use the five garbage bags full for decorating his shop. The 'Mountain Queen', a magnificent saxifrage, is even on the highest peak never safe from the persistent attempts of Tor Gundersen to reach it – even barefoot if he doesn't happen to have his climbing boots with him. Masses of goldenrod, meadow-sweet, and liverwort, the first of the year – he knows where to find them all. But it's no wonder that, after twenty years of experience, he has discovered secret places all over the country. Never does he come home empty-handed. For example there was that water lily pond near Oslo. He discovered it coincidentally in the spring and when the idea for a water creation developed in the summer, he went out and bought an inflatable rubber boat, paddled it out on the pond and gathered the lilies and leaves. Bloodsuckers and such don't bother him a bit. And a day later the sidewalk outside his flower shop in Oslo was crowded with people jostling to get a look at his display window...

# 花材捜索

### 頑強な & 情熱的な

道端でいつも青く輝く何かを目にし、すぐに確認できない時、ブレーキが音をたてます。これはちょっと調べてみないと！最終的には今まで見た事のない花、次の製作へのベースとなるかもしれません。未熟者には高速道路わきのグリーンが生い茂った防壁は退屈でしょうが、花材を見つけ出すマイスターは苦もなく、そこに密集したフキタンポポを見つけ出します。そして停車禁止地帯へと繋がる道を見出します。チャンスだ、一度にこんなにたくさん！ごみ袋五袋分いっぱいの収穫物を店舗装飾にどのようにして利用するかはもちろんすでに計算済みです。見事な多肉植物"Felsenkönigin"(岩の女王)、大文字草はトゥル・グンダーセンが必死に壁を攀じ登ろうとしても安全ではない目のくらむような高い位置に生息します。トレッキングシューズが手元にないときは裸足で攀じ登るほどです。たくさんのアキノキリンソウ　（セイタカアワダチソウ）、シモツケソウ、スハマソウ。彼はそれらが1年で最も早く目に出来る場所を知っています。20年の経験からそれらの場所を知り尽くしているのは不思議な事ではなく、手ぶらで帰ることなどありません。そしてオスロ近郊には睡蓮の咲く池もあります。彼は春に偶然その池を発見し、夏のウォーターオブジェクトのアイディアが浮かびました。彼はゴムボートを購入し、そのボートを漕ぎながら花と葉を収穫しました。蛭やその他の生き物なんて気になりません。翌日、鼻がペシャンコになった旅行者がオスロの窓際でこっそり姿を消すことでしょう。

# KARRIERE

## Zielstrebig & selbstbewusst

Es gibt Menschen, die sind glücklich und zufrieden mit einem gleichmäßig dahinplätschernden Leben. Tor Gundersen gehört definitiv nicht dazu. Er könnte nicht sein Leben lang jeden Tag das Gleiche tun. Es spuken viel zu viele Ideen in seinem Kopf, die verwirklicht werden wollen. Viele Jahre hat er gelernt, in Blumengeschäften gearbeitet, die Basis für den Beruf geschaffen. Parallel dazu nahm er fleißig an floristischen Wettbewerben teil. Unzählige Medaillen und Pokale zeugen von seinem Einsatz, der schon extrem zu nennen ist, sodass die letzte Trophäe dieses Aufstiegs, der Europacup, gerade zur richtigen Zeit den krönenden Schlusspunkt setzte. Kurz zuvor hatte er sich als freiberuflicher Florist selbstständig gemacht, die Nachfrage nach Demonstrationen, Jurytätigkeit, Unterrichten und vielem mehr war groß. Nach dem Europacup stieg sie ins Unvorstellbare. Mehr als 200 Tage pro Jahr war er seitdem rund um den Globus auf Achse! Doch auch dies allein würde er nicht ewig weitermachen, das war klar. Außerdem wollte er Publikum gewinnen. Als sich

die Gelegenheit bot einen Blumenladen in Oslo zu kaufen, griff er zu. Nun muss man nicht meinen, dass er die Reisetätigkeit deswegen aufgegeben hätte! Es sind immer noch 130 Tage im Jahr, die seine Mitarbeiter ohne ihn auskommen müssen. Der Ansatz zu einer anderen, ausbaufähigen Entwicklung war das mit Geschäftspartnerin Kiko Zimmerman gegründete Unternehmen „tk concepts", das seltene, gute Produkte und ein Kursprogramm für Floristen anbietet. Von den ersten Wettbewerbserfolgen zum internationalen Star der Floristenszene - das nenne ich eine Karriere. Das Überraschende ist, dass Tor keine Karriere geplant hat, sondern immer das tat, was seine Gestalterseele ihm vorgab, oft gegen Widerstände, vor allem aber schlicht mit harter Arbeit. Jeder Erfolg bestärkte ihn weiterzuführen, woran er glaubte. So wird der Junge von der kleinen Insel „Runde" an der Westküste Norwegens auch weiterhin neue, große Schritte wagen. Was? Wer weiß das schon!

nordisk blomster-
...ester fra Ulsteinvik

*„Tor, du brenner ditt lys i begge ender!!!"* *(„Tor, du zündest deine Kerze von beiden Seiten an!!!", nach dem norwegischen Sprichwort, das Menschen beschreibt, die ohne Atempause planen, am liebsten immer mehrere Projekte gleichzeitig.)*

Turid Gundersen (Norwegen), Tors Mutter

# CAREER

### Single-minded & self-confident

There are people who are happy and satisfied leading a calm and uneventful life. Tor Gundersen is definitely not one of them. He could never imagine doing the same thing every day for the rest of his life. There are too many ideas racing around in his head that need to be put into practice. For many years he studied the basics of floristry, then worked in a flower shop to build up the basis for working in his chosen profession. And at the same time he actively participated in floristic competitions. Countless medals and cups attest to his commitment – which anyone would consider extreme. His most recent trophy – the Europe Cup – was the crowning glory in his high-flying career at just the right time. Shortly before winning it he had started working as a freelance florist, and he was in great demand for demonstrations, jury duty, lessons and much more. But after the Europe Cup things escalated to unimaginable proportions: he began travelling all over the world, spending more than 200 days a year on tour! But it was clear that he wouldn't keep on doing this forever. And besides, he wanted to enhance his image in the public eye. So when the chance to buy his own shop in Oslo came along, he jumped for it. But don't think for a moment that he has stopped travelling because of that! He still averages around 130 days a year on the road – while his staff has to get by without him. Then a new idea for a business with potential for expansion became "tk concepts", the company that he founded with Kiko Zimmerman for supplying florists with rare, high quality products for their creations as well as a teaching program. From title-holding champion to international star of the florist scene in leaps and bounds – now that's what I call a career! The surprising thing is that Tor never planned his career, but rather always did what his artistic soul dictated – often against all odds, and always with a lot of hard work. And every success gives him the strength to continue doing what he believes in. This likeable young man from the small island of Runde on the west coast of Norway will continue to forge amazing new paths. Where will they lead to? Who knows!

*"Tor, du brenner ditt lys i begge ender!!!" ("Tor, you're burning your candle at both ends!!!", a Norwegian saying for describing people who make plans without a moment's rest, preferably several projects at once.)*

Turid Gundersen (Norway), Tor's mother

# キャリアー

### 目標に向かってひたすら努力する & 自意識のある

単調な生活に幸せを感じ、満足している人々がいます。トゥルー・グンダーセンは勿論そうではなく、生涯を通じて毎日同じ事ができないのかもしれません。実現したいアイディアが絶え間なく彼の頭の中を駆け巡ります。長年、学び、花店に従事し、プロへの基礎を作り上げ、それと同時にフローリストの競技会にも参加しました。数え切れないほどのメダルとカップは彼の活躍を物語っています。その結果、まさに相応しい時期にヨーロッパカップのトロフィーを手にしたわけですが、その直前には、フリーランスのフローリストとして活動しはじめていたのです。デモンストレーション、競技会の審査員、講義への問い合わせ…ヨーロッパカップ後は想像もつかないほど忙しくなり、それからというもの、1年を通じて200日以上地球上のあらゆる土地を旅しています。もちろんそれを永く続けられないことは判りきっていました。彼は理解を得たかったのです。オスロで花店を購入する機会を提供されたとき、彼はその提供を受け入れました。ここで彼が旅する事を断念するだろうと考えてはいけません！今なお1年の内130日は彼の従業員が花店を切り盛りしなければなりません。ビジネスパートナー・紀公子ジィママンとの企画が今後の有望な展開の発端となり、それはフローリストにとって稀有で魅力的なものでした。プロにとって大舞台である国際競技会での成功をキャリアーと言えるでしょう。意外な事にトゥルー・グンダーセンはキャリアーを期待せず、彼の芸術家精神は自身にもたらすことのみを常に追求してきました。しかしそれは厳しい作業であると同時に、時として障害となりました。それぞれの成功が彼を前進させるものと信じていました。こうして、西ノルウェーの小さなルンド島出身の若者は、依然として新しい、大きな前進を試みています。それが何か？もうおわかりでしょう！

「トゥルー、蝋燭を両側から灯しているわ！」ノルウェーの諺より-
息つく間もなく計画し、たくさんのプロジェクトを同時にすることを好む人物の意。

トゥリッド グンダーセン（ノルウェー）：トゥルーの母

# DEMONSTRATIONEN

Großer Auftritt: Hochzeitsshow mit Kiko
vor Fachpublikum in Boston/USA (1997)

Big performance: wedding show with Kiko
for professional florists in Boston/USA (1997)

大舞台: 紀公子ジィママンとの専門家向けブ
ライダルショー アメリカ・ボストン (1997)

Kleine Demo: Gastflorist für einen Tag im
Floralstudio Salzmann, Åros/Norwegen (1998)

Small demo: guest florist for a day in the
floral studio Salzmann, Åros/Norway (1998)

小さなデモ: ノルウェー・オーロス フローラルスタ
ジオ・ザルツマンにて一日フローリスト (1998)

## Konzentriert & charismatisch

Es fing damit an, dass Tor Gundersen mit etwa
fünfundzwanzig Jahren die Oslo-Meisterschaft,
kurz danach die Skandinavien-Meisterschaft, seinen ersten internationalen Wettbewerb, gewann
und daraufhin als Teilnehmer zum Weltcup nach
Tokio geschickt wurde. Das war ein bisschen zu
früh, als dass man dort hätte große Erfolge erwar-
ten können. Doch die Japaner wurden aufmerk-
sam, wollten ein Buch mit Tor Gundersen machen.
Zum Erscheinen organisierten sie eine Fachde-
monstration, die große Beachtung fand. Es folgten
Anfragen aus Taiwan und anderen Teilen der Welt.
Das Schneeballsystem begann. Sein Europacup-
Sieg in Deutschland brachte einen zweiten Schub
an Einladungen, die ihm internationales Arbeiten
ermöglichten. Heute sind es bereits über zwanzig
Länder, in denen Tor Gundersen gern gesehener
Gastdozent war, und der Strom reißt nicht ab.
Was sich so locker beschreiben lässt, ist in Wahrheit
allerdings eine unglaublich harte Knochenarbeit:
Ständig andere Menschen und Mentalitäten, un-
bekannte Orte und Materialien, allein das ist schon

anstrengend. In Deutschland jedenfalls waren
Helfer und Assistenten immer sehr schnell ihrer
romantischen Vorstellung beraubt und dafür tief
beeindruckt, wenn sie auch nur am Rande mitbeka-
men, was Tor Gundersen in diesem Job alles leistet.
Dass er hochkonzentriert und diszipliniert bei der
Sache ist und es trotzdem schafft, eine lockere
Arbeitsatmosphäre zu erhalten, überrascht immer
wieder. Dass er jeden im Team mit gleichem Respekt
behandelt und vom Konzept bis zur letzten Drah-
tung alles verständlich erklärt, hat ihm zudem viel
Dankbarkeit beschert. Die gleiche Haltung ist es,
die seine charismatische Ausstrahlung auf der
Bühne bestimmt. Die Zuschauer spüren, dass die-
ser Mensch sie offen und ehrlich an seinen gestalterischen Gedanken teilhaben lässt. Sie empfinden,
dass er hier nicht nur einen Job macht, sondern
eine perfektionistische Arbeit aus Passion. Wird
diese verstanden und geschätzt, ist das das größte
Kompliment für Tor Gundersen.

# DEMONSTRATIONS

## デモンストレーション

### Focussed & charismatic

It all began when Tor Gundersen won the Oslo championships at the age of 25, shortly after he had won the Scandinavian Championship, his first international competition, after which he was sent to Tokyo to participate in the World Cup. Unfortunately it was a bit too soon to expect a major success there, but the Japanese floristry community was nevertheless very impressed with Tor Gundersen and wanted to do a book with him. The presentation of the book was then organized with a demonstration for professional florists, who paid it considerable respect. Numerous inquiries followed from Taiwan and other parts of the world. The snowballing process had begun. His Europe Cup victory in Germany triggered a second wave of invitations, which led to more work in the international arena. By now already over twenty countries have welcomed Tor Gundersen as a guest lecturer – and there is no sign of the flow ebbing anytime soon.

Although it may sound relatively easy, in reality there is a lot of unbelievably hard work involved. The constant confrontation with other people and other mentalities, foreign places and new materials alone can be very tiring. In any case, his helpers and assistants in Germany soon lost their romantic visions and were deeply impressed – even if only partially involved – with all that Tor Gundersen has to do in his job. He is a study in constant motion: throwing himself into his work with the highest level of concentration and discipline, while at the same time maintaining a relaxed working atmosphere, he is a never-ending source of surprise and delight to those around him. The way he treats everyone in the team with the same measure of respect and takes the time to explain everything from the concept down to the last wiring detail in a way that everyone can understand has also added to his popularity. It is the same manner that makes him so charismatic on stage. His public senses that this person is open and honest, and that he wants to share with them his creative thoughts and ideas. They instinctively feel that for him it is not just a job, but rather perfectionist work full of passion. And if this message is understood and appreciated, for Tor Gundersen it is the highest compliment of all.

### 集中した & カリスマ的な

トゥルー・グンダーセンは25歳の時にオスロチャンピオンとなり、その後間もなく初の国際競技会で勝利を収めスカンジナビアチャンピオンとなりました。その結果東京で開催されるワールドカップの参加者に選出されたのです。当時、大きな成功を期待するには少々早過ぎるようでした。しかし、日本人は彼に注目し、作品集を出版することを申し出、その出版記念に専門家向けのデモンストレーションを企画しました。その後台湾を始め世界中のあらゆる所からの問い合わせが殺到し、雪合戦のシステムが始まりました。ドイツで開催されたヨーロッパカップでの勝利が2度目の国際的な活動へと急速に導きました。今日では既に20カ国以上の国々でトゥルー・グンダーセンを好意的に客員講師として迎え、その熱が醒める事はありません。

安易に描写することはできても、実際にはとんでもない重労働です。絶え間ない人付き合いと様々なメンタリティー、見知らぬ土地、材料、それだけでも体力を消耗させます。ドイツでは少なくとも協力者やアシスタントは、すぐに自分たちのロマンティックなイメージが変えられ、トゥルー・グンダーセンが成し遂げるものすべてに深い感銘を受けるのです。彼はある状態に非常に集中しながらも和やかな雰囲気をかもし出します。彼はどの仕事仲間であれ同等に敬意を払い、コンセプトから最後まですべてを解りやすく説明する、それは彼にとって大きなやりがいとなります。この姿勢は彼のステージ上でのカリスマ的な輝きと等しいでしょう。聴衆はこの人物が自分達と彼の芸術的観念を正直に分かち合っていることを感じ、彼がただ作業しているだけではなく、その作業が情熱から生まれていることを体感するでしょう。これこそトゥルー・グンダーセンへの最大の賛辞なのです。

# ROSEN-SHOW

Berauschender Schlussakkord: Tor und Solveig und die Rose (Oslo, 1996)
Grand finale: Tor and Solveig with The Rose (Oslo, 1996)
うっとりするような最後の旋律: トゥルー、スルヴェイそしてバラ (オスロ 1996)

Stimmungsvoll: Einladungskarte zu „Dans på Roser" (Oslo, 1996)
Suspenseful: invitation to "Dans på Roser" (Oslo, 1996)
雰囲気ある: "Dans på Roser"の招待状 (オスロ 1996)

## Einfühlsam & sinnlich

Das Leben, wissen wir alle, ist nicht nur eitel Sonnenschein oder, wie die Norweger sagen, ein „dans på roser" (Tanz auf Rosen). Umso wichtiger erscheint es, dass wir uns im Leben so viel Freude wie möglich bereiten. Tor Gundersen hatte genau das zum Thema einer wundervollen, einzigartigen Inszenierung gemacht: ein Bühnenstück im alten Osloer Theater, bei dem sich alles um die Rose dreht. Rosen regnen herab und aus den Blütenbergen erheben sich Tänzer zum Ballett. Auftritt von Solveig und Tor, die zu sanfter Musik florale Kreationen fertigen - natürlich aus Rosen, Rosen, Rosen. Künstler treten auf. Das Märchen von „Dornröschen" wird vorgetragen, Rosen-Gedichte werden rezitiert. Musik vom "Rosenkavalier" bis zu norwegischen Volksweisen ist Teil der spektaku-lären Aktionen auf der Bühne. Das Publikum ist mal laut begeistert, mal still berührt, je nach Darbietung. Auch so manche Träne rollt. Dann atemberaubende Dramatik zum Schluss. Eine Stimme spricht: „Das Leben kann ein 'Tanz auf Rosen' sein, aber vergiss nicht, dass Rosen auch Dornen haben." Vor dem Rosenzaun in blauem Licht bindet Tor aus zunächst undefinierbaren, gewölbten Teilen eine Art Strauß in der Hand, steckt die fertige Form auf ein hohes Stahlrohr, an dem unübersehbar ein großer Metall-Dorn prangt. Jetzt erkennt das Publikum die riesige Rose. Was für ein Applaus! Übrigens: Was da samtig-rot wie eine Rose aussieht, ist tatsächlich eine Rose. Genauer gesagt Staub aus getrockneten und gemahlenen Rosenblütenblättern...

*„Nur ein Satz: Ich bewundere Tors Art und Weise zu arbeiten, seinen Respekt im Umgang mit der Blume und sein besonderes Gefühl für ihre Bewegung."*

Solveig Haugen Andersen (Norwegen), ehemalige Arbeitgeberin von Tor, Partnerin bei diversen Projekten

# ROSE SHOW

### Sensitive & sensual

As we all know, life is not always a bed of roses, as the Norwegians say, a "dans på roser" (dance on roses). All the more reason to make sure we get as much enjoyment as possible out of life. Based on exactly this theme, Tor Gundersen staged a wonderful and unique performance in the old Oslo theater, with the rose as star of the show. Imagine this: roses rain down on the stage and dancers arise from underneath mountains of flower petals to perform their ballet. Solveig and Tor appear and create floral arrangements to the strains of soft music – naturally with roses, roses, and more roses. Actors interpret the fairy tale "Sleeping Beauty" and poems about roses are recited. The music from "Rosenkavalier" and Norwegian folk songs are among the spectacular events on the stage that night. The public responds with everything from thundering applause to quiet emotion. More than a few tears are shed. Then the breathtaking grand finale – a voice announces: "Life can be a 'dance on roses' but do not forget that roses also have thorns." In front of a rose trellis bathed in blue light, Tor begins binding a kind of bouquet of curved elements that at first cannot be identified, then displays the finished creation with a flourish on a tall metal pole embellished with an unmistakable large metal thorn. Suddenly the audience recognizes the oversized rose. Enthusiastic applause erupts! Incidentally: the velvety red rose construction is not entirely fake. Its huge "petals" are covered with dried and ground up rose petals...

*"Just one sentence: I admire the way Tor works, the respect he has for flowers and plants and his special feeling for their movement."*

Solveig Haugen Andersen (Norway), former employer of Tor and partner in various projects

# ローズショー

### 思いやりある & 感覚的な

人生は太陽が輝くだけではないことを私達は知っています。あるいは、ノルウェー人が言う"バラの上のダンス"ということを。生きていく上で、出来るだけ多くの喜びを分かちあうことは重要なことです。トゥルー・グンダーセンはこのテーマを見事に、類いなく演出しました。古いオスロ劇場の舞台の一角すべてをバラで囲んだのです。バラが舞い落ち、その積もった花びらの中からダンサー達が立ち上がるのです。花の創作品が穏やかな音楽を創り出すというスルヴァイとトゥルーの演出もちろん、バラ、バラ、バラ。メルヘン"いばら姫"が朗読され、バラの詩が朗誦されます。"ローゼン カヴァリェ"(ヨハン・シュトラウスのオペレッタ)に始まり、ノルウェー民謡に至る音楽は好奇心をあおります。観客は演目によって時には騒々しく、時には心ひそかに感動し、多くの観客は涙を流すのです。そして息をのむドラマチックなクライマックス。劇中、こう語られます「人生は"バラの上のダンス"であるかもしれません。でも忘れないで下さい、バラには棘もあることを」青い光に照らされたバラの垣根の前で、トゥルーはアーチ型の花束を手にし、大きな鉄製の棘が輝くスチールパイプ上に刺すのです。拍手喝采！赤く見えるものは実はバラなのです。より厳密に言えば花粉。乾燥し、粉々になったバラの花びら、バラの葉っぱ…

「一言だけ。花と花の動きをとらえる彼の特別な感覚と、周囲の人々に気を配るトゥルーの作業方法には驚嘆します。」

スルヴェイ・ハウゲン・アンダーセン(ノルウェー):かつてのトゥルーの雇用者、種々のプロジェクトのパートナー

# LADEN

Schmuckstück: Tors Laden in Oslo,
Eingang Ullevålsveien (2000)

Rare jewel: Tor's shop in Oslo,
street entrance on Ullevålsveien (2000)

装飾の一部分: オスロにあるトゥルーの店舗、
ウレヴォルスヴェイン入り口 (2000)

Platzwechsel: Die Seerosen landen im
Schaufenster (2000)

Change of scenery: the water lilies land
in the display window (2000)

模様替え: 睡蓮、ショーウィンドウへの登場 (2000)

## Klar & konsequent

Einen eigenen Laden zu eröffnen ist eine aufregende Sache. Besonders, wenn man zwar in der Branche einen großen Namen hat, aber gar nicht sicher sein kann, ob das im Kollegenkreis so geschätzte Floraldesign beim Kunden ebenso gut ankommen wird. Doch Tor Gundersen wäre nicht Tor Gundersen, wenn er bei dem Konzept für ein eigenes Geschäft nicht mit der gleichen Leidenschaft und Akribie vorginge wie bei allen anderen beruflichen Aktivitäten. Alles soll zusammenpassen. So kann die Ausrichtung des Ladens nur eine logische Fortführung des bestehenden Images sein – Corporate Identity im besten Sinn. Und wirklich – ein Blick ins Schaufenster oder ins Ladeninnere genügt, dass die, die seine Arbeit kennen, sofort sagen würden, das ist er, ganz eindeutig. Aber auch Passanten und Kunden sprangen von Anfang an auf die eigenwillige Atmosphäre aus Alt und Neu, aus traditionellen Elementen und futuristischen Floralobjekten an. Es liegt vielleicht daran, dass jeder Bereich und jedes Teil, ob Wandfarben oder Bodenbelag, Vasen oder Blumen, Warenträger oder Ein-

packpapier, eine klare Zuordnung zum Ganzen erkennen lässt. Es gibt ausgesuchte Schnittblumen vom Markt ebenso wie einzelne botanische Raritäten aus dem Garten, aber immer auch Gesammeltes aus der Natur: Kiefern im Winter, Gräser und Wildblumen im Sommer. Jedes noch so kleine Ding wird so präsentiert, dass seine spezifischen Eigenheiten als besonders wertvoll betont werden, und der Kunde spürt und erkennt die Bedeutung. Bei dem ausgeprägten Individualismus in seiner Gestaltung musste Tor Gundersen vorher Zweifel haben, ob es genügend Leute geben würde, die die richtige Antenne dafür haben. Noch vor wenigen Jahren hatte er selbstkritisch geäußert: „Manchmal denke ich, wenn ich einen Laden hätte, ginge ich wahrscheinlich bankrott, vielleicht erwarte ich zu viel von den Kunden." Welch ein Glück, dass er sich irrte!

*„Es war eine Begegnung wie mit einer Sternschnuppe: kurz, aber leuchtend, intensiv und tief beeindruckend. Ein Moment des Erkennens und Verstehens. Ich habe selten jemanden erlebt, der so klar umrissene Vorstellungen von seiner Lebensart hat und diese so konsequent und stimmig umsetzt wie Tor. Pur wie Quellwasser, unverfälscht, von natürlicher Eleganz. Seine Einstellung zur Floristik ergibt sich beinahe zwingend daraus und umgekehrt kann man aus seiner floristischen Arbeit Rückschlüsse auf seine Persönlichkeit ziehen. Kurz: Versteht man seine Floristik, versteht man auch den Menschen Tor Gundersen!"*

Evi Gerull (Deutschland), Floristin und Lehrerin, Teilnehmerin und Assistentin von Tor auf Kreuzfahrt-Seminar in Norwegen

# SHOP

### Clear & consistent

Opening up your own flower shop is a very exciting event. Especially if you have already made a name for yourself in the business but cannot be completely sure if the floral design your colleagues so admire will also be a hit with everyday customers. But Tor Gundersen wouldn't be Tor Gundersen if he didn't apply the same meticulous care and passion to the concept for his own shop as to all of his other professional activities. Everything has to match. It is the only way for the style of his shop to become the logical continuation of his existing image – corporate identity in the true sense of the word. And it worked – one glance in the display window or the interior of the shop will tell anyone who is familiar with his work right away: yes that's Tor alright, no doubt about it. But even passers-by and customers went for the unique atmosphere from day one – a combination of old and new, of tradition and elements and futuristic floral objects. Perhaps because in every nook and cranny – be it the colour of the walls or the floor covering, the vases or flowers, display shelves or wrapping paper – one can clearly see that each individual element is a part of the whole. There are carefully selected cut flowers from the market alongside single botanical rarities from the garden, as well as elements gathered from the nature that is typically Norway: pines in winter, grasses and wild flowers in summer. Even the smallest object is presented in a way that underscores the value of its specific qualities and the customer senses and recognizes the significance. With a creative design so full of distinctive individualism, Tor Gundersen must really have wondered whether enough people would be on the same wavelength. Only a few years ago he criticized himself, saying: "Sometimes I think that if I had my own shop I'd probably go broke. Maybe I expect too much of my customers." How lucky we are that he was wrong!

*"It was like an encounter with a shooting star – brief but dazzling, intensive and deeply impressive. A moment of recognition and understanding. I have seldom met anyone who has such a clearly defined vision of his lifestyle and who so consistently and fascinatingly implements it as Tor does. Pure as spring water, authentic, blessed with a natural elegance. These qualities have created his attitude towards his floristry and, conversely, one can recognize his personality in his work. In a word: anyone who understands his floristry also understands Tor Gundersen the person!"*

Evi Gerull (Germany), florist and teacher, participant and assistant to Tor on cruise ship seminars in Norway

# 店舗

### クリアーな & 一貫性ある

その分野で特に名が通っている場合、自身の店を開店することは興奮するものです。しかし、その同僚が顧客の期待するフラワーデザインを提供できるかどうかはわかりません。他の活動と同じく、変わらぬ情熱と極度の細心さを持たない店舗をコンセプトにしていたら、トゥルー・グンダーセンはトゥルー・グンダーセンではないかもしれません。すべてが一致しなければならず、花店を営むということは存在するイメージを論理的に継続することなのです。同じ価値観を抱く者達の協力。実際、彼の作品を知る人々がショーウィンドーや店内にある作品を見れば、それらが彼のものであることは一目瞭然でしょう。そして通行人や顧客は古いものから新しいものへの癖のある雰囲気、伝統的な要素から未来風フラワーオブジェクトに視線を向けました。もしかすると、壁の色や床材、花器や花材、配達人や包装紙など、ひとつひとつの要素が他との違いをはっきりと示しているのかもしれません。市場で選ばれた切花もあれば、庭から摘んだ稀少植物、でもこれらの収集物はすべて自然の産物です。冬には松を、夏には野生の花など。彼の繊細さが展示され、顧客はその意図を感じ、理解するのです。以前、トゥルー・グンダーセンは自身の作品の個性に疑念を抱きました。果たしてどれだけの人が作品を理解してくれるのだろうかと。数年前彼は自己批判しました。「時にこう思うことがあります。もし私が店を構えていたら、おそらく破産して、顧客から多くのことを期待していたかもしれません。」思い違いをしたなんて、なんてラッキーなのでしょう！

「流れ星を見つけたような出会いでした。ほんのひと時でしたが、輝いた、深い印象を受けました。一瞬でお互いを理解しました。自身の生活様式にそんなにはっきりとしたイメージを持った人物に出会うのはそうめったにないことだからです。トゥルーのように徹底していて、調和がとれていることは稀な事です。泉のように純粋で、自然な上品さ。彼のフロリスティックに対する態度はすべてそこから生まれているのです。逆に言えば、彼の作品が彼の個性を引き出す鍵であることもわかるでしょう。最後に一言。彼のフロリスティックを理解すると同時に、トゥルー・グンダーセンという人物をも理解するのです！」

エヴィ・ゲルル(ドイツ):フローリスト、講師、トゥルーのノルウェー十字軍セミナー参加者・アシスタント

# KÖNIGLICHE HOCHZEIT

Traumhaft: das Kronprinzenpaar im floral geschmückten Dom (Oslo, 2001)

A dream: the Crown Prince and his bride in the florally decorated cathedral (Oslo, 2001)

夢のような: 皇太子夫妻 花で装飾された大聖堂にて (オスロ 2000)

Geduldsarbeit: Huflattich-Segel am Kirchenportal (Oslo, 2001)

Painstaking work: coltsfoot sails in front of the church (Oslo, 2001)

忍耐強く: 正面玄関フキタンポポの帆 (オスロ 2000)

## Bescheiden & professionell

Ist es Schicksal oder Glück? In jedem Fall ist es eine große Ehre und Anerkennung der beruflichen Leistungen, wenn ein Florist bei einem solchen Ereignis mit nationaler Bedeutung um seine Mitarbeit gefragt wird. Tor Gundersen war einer aus dem Team von vier Floristen, dem die Blumendekoration für die Kronprinzenhochzeit von Norwegen übertragen wurde. Die Aufgaben waren klar verteilt, von administrativen Arbeiten bis zur Materialbeschaffung. Tor war der Designer, der Formgeber. Und welch eine glückliche Fügung, dass die Vorstellungen des Brautpaares und des Königshauses sich so wunderbar mit Tors minimalistischer Ader deckten! Schlicht und für eine Königliche Hochzeit ungewöhnlich volksnah war die ganze Hochzeitszeremonie angelegt, die die Einfachheit jedoch würdevoll und feierlich erscheinen ließ. Ebenso schlicht präsentierte sich der Blumenschmuck vor und in der Kirche, am Schloss und anderen Gebäuden: schlicht, aber nicht unscheinbar, auffällig,

aber nicht aufdringlich. Zeitlos sollte die Formensprache sein und so entstanden meist unifarbige Kugeln und Kegel aus Rosen oder Rentierflechte, Blättern oder Früchten, Girlanden aus Schleierkraut, dreieckige Segelobjekte aus geklebten Huflattichblättern. Viele Produkte der heimischen Flora wurden verwendet, allen voran die Heide, die Nationalblume Norwegens, die zum Beispiel – unübersehbar – in drei Meter hohe Vasenformen eingeflochten wurde. Vielleicht ist es eine allgemeine norwegische Eigenschaft mit wenigen Mitteln effektiv zu sein und etwas Wesentliches zu zeigen. Dann ist Tor Gundersen, was Floraldesign betrifft, sicher der deutlichste Vertreter. Übrigens: Das Königshaus war auch sehr zufrieden mit dem Ergebnis. Und was für eine Freude am Ende der Recherchen für das vorliegende Buch noch ein solches Highlight in das Porträt von Tor Gundersen aufnehmen zu können!

# ROYAL WEDDING

### Modest & professional

Was it fate or good luck? In any case it is a great honour and acknowledgement of his professional achievements when a florist is asked to be part of an event of such national importance. Tor Gundersen was one of a team of four florists who were in charge of supplying the floral decorations for the wedding of Norway's Crown Prince and his bride. The spheres of responsibility were clearly demarcated, from the administrative work to the selection and purchasing of the materials. Tor was the floral designer, in charge of the overall concept. And what an act of providence that the ideas of the bride and groom and those of the royal family so perfectly coincided with Tor's minimalist style! A simple and elegant wedding ceremony with a common touch unusual for a royal wedding, but with a simplicity that was both worthy and festive. Equally simple was the presentation of the floral decorations around and inside the church, at the royal palace and other buildings – simple but not too modest, noticeable but not too overdone. The aim was for a timeless design, which was expressed by mostly monochrome balls of roses or reindeer moss, leaves and fruit, garlands of gypsophila, three-cornered sails of glued coltsfoot leaves. Many products of domestic flora were used, in particular heather, the national flower of Norway, which for example – a real eye-catcher – was woven into three-meter tall vases. Perhaps it is a general Norwegian custom to make an effective but essential statement with few materials. In that case Tor Gundersen, with respect to floral design, is surely a good representative of his country. And incidentally: the royal family was also very satisfied with the results. And what a pleasure for me, at the end of my research for this book, to be able to include such a highlight in the portrait of Tor Gundersen!

*"When Tor started working for me in 1985, he was so slow that he made me quite nervous. I didn't want to push him too much because I like it when the floral assemblies are made with care. But I had no choice. What can I say – he understood right away! And when he left after almost three years he was putting things together quickly and with great capability. I have never seen such a fast florist…"*

Guro Fjell (Norway), former employer of Tor, active member of the Florists' Association

# 王室婚礼

### 慎ましく & プロフェッショナルに

運命か幸福か？一人のフローリストが重要な国民行事に協力を求められることは、偉大な名誉であり、高く評価されることです。トゥルー・グンダーセンはノルウェー王室婚礼の花材装飾を委ねられた４人のフローリストチームの一人でした。その任務は行政上の作業から材料の調達まではっきりと区別されました。トゥルーはデザイナー。新郎新婦と王室のイメージがトゥルーの素晴らしいミニマリズムと一致するなんて！その構想は王室婚礼が控えめながらも品位を備え、国民に親しみやすく、荘厳に執り行なわれるということでした。そこで教会、宮殿を始めとする建物内でもそのように装飾されました。控えめ、しかし目立たないのではなく、著しくもなく、しつこくもなく。時の流れにとらわれない形。そこでバラや花苔、葉や実でできた単一色の球や円錐、かすみ草のガーランド、フキタンポポの葉が貼り付けられた三角型の帆のオブジェ。故郷の植物がたくさんの作品に用いられました。なかでも、ノルウェーの国花であるエリカは３ｍもある花器の形に編みこまれ、見渡せないほどでした。数少ない材料で効果的に、本質を示すというのはノルウェーの一般的な特徴なのかもしれません。トゥルー・グンダーセンは花をデザインし、その特徴を示すのです。王室もその成果にとても満足でした。そしてなんと言う喜びでしょう！この作品集の最終の取材段階でトゥルー・グンダーセンのハイライトを取り上げる事ができるとは！

「1985年にトゥルーが私の店で働き始めたとき、私がかなりナーバスになるほど彼はゆっくりしていました。作品が一つ一つきちんと仕上げられるのを好んでいたので、駆り立てることはしませんでした。どう言うべきでしょう、彼はそれをわかっていたのです！約3年後に彼が私の元を去ったとき、手速く、完璧に仕上げられていました。そんなに覚えの速いフローリストに出会ったことはありません…」

ギュロ・フィエル(ノルウェー)：かつてのトゥルーの雇用者、フローリスト連盟にて活躍

# WERKE
# WORKS
# 作品集

# DIE GEFÄSSFORM FORTSETZEN

# CONTINUATION OF CONTAINERS

器の継続

花器: アールデコの器-ローズヴィル/アメリカ、平面型
花材: フクシア、ツバカズラ属-japonica

VASE: Art Deco-Vase aus Roseville/USA, abgeflachte Form
MATERIAL: Fuchsia, *Fallopia japonica* (syn. *Reynoutria*)

VASE: Art Deco vase from Roseville/USA, flat form
MATERIAL: Fuchsia, *Fallopia japonica* (syn. *Reynoutria*)

花器: アールデコの器-ローズヴィル/アメリカ、平面型
花材: フクシア、ツバカズラ属-japonica

VASE: Keramikvase von Sandra Rich/Deutschland
MATERIAL: *Artemisia vulgaris, Solidago virgaurea,*
*Anthurium crassinervum* (Blüten und Blätter)


VASE: ceramic vase by Sandra Rich/Germany
MATERIAL: *Artemisia vulgaris, Solidago virgaurea,*
*Anthurium crassinervum* (flowers and leaves)


花器: 陶器-サンドラ・リッチ社/ドイツ
花材: ヨモギ属-vulgaris、アキノキリンソウ属-virgaurea、
アンスリウム-crassinervum(花弁・葉)

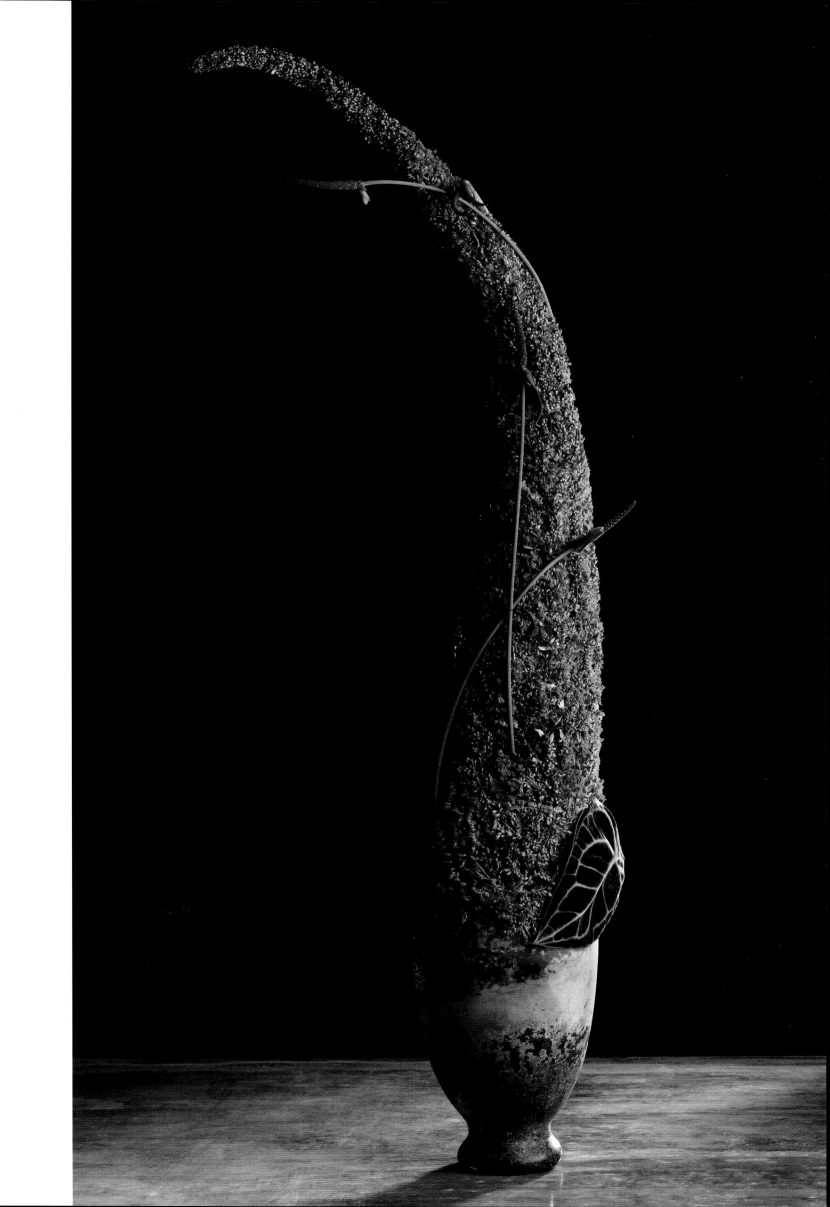

花器: 韓国産陶器、サルビアグリーン釉油塗り
花材: 芍薬-lactiflora、フキタンポポ属-farfara、昼顔-arvensis

VASE:  Koreanische Keramik mit typischer salbeigrüner
Craquelé-Glasur
MATERIAL:  *Paeonia lactiflora, Tussilago farfara,*
*Convolvulus arvensis*


VASE:  Korean sageware with typical sage-green crackle glaze
MATERIAL:  *Paeonia lactiflora, Tussilago farfara,*
*Convolvulus arvensis*


花器: 韓国産陶器、サルビアグリーン釉油塗り
花材: 芍薬-lactiflora、フキタンポポ属-farfara、昼顔-arvensis

VASE: Französische Eisenurne (Reproduktion)
MATERIAL: *Rumex longifolius, Passiflora x violacea, Amaranthus caudatus, Scadoxus multiflorus* subsp. *katherinae* (syn. *Haemanthus katheriae*), *Allium sphaerocephalon, Zantedeschia rehmannii, Helianthus annuus, Rubus fruticosus, Eremurus robustus*

VASE: French iron urn (reproduction)
MATERIAL: *Rumex longifolius, Passiflora x violacea, Amaranthus caudatus, Scadoxus multiflorus* subsp. *katherinae* (syn. *Haemanthus katheriae*), *Allium sphaerocephalon, Zantedeschia rehmannii, Helianthus annuus, Rubus fruticosus, Eremurus robustus*

花器: フランス産鉄製壷(複製)
花材: たで科-longifolius、時計草属-x violacea、アマランサス-caudatus、ヒガンバナ科-multiflorus、アリウム-sphaerocephalon、サトイモ科-rehmannii、ヒマワリ属-annuus、木苺属-fruticosus、エルムレス-robustus

GEFÄSS: Keramik aus Korea
MATERIAL: *Fritillaria meleagris, Rhizophora mangle* (= Mangrove)


CONTAINER: Korean pottery
MATERIAL: *Fritillaria meleagris, Rhizophora mangle* (= mangrove)


花器: 陶器(韓国)
花材: フリチラリア-meleagris、マングローブ-mangle

**VASE:** Chinesische Keramik
**MATERIAL:** *Rosa* 'Sahara', *Betula* (Zweige), *Triticum aestivum*


**VASE:** Chinese pottery
**MATERIAL:** *Rosa* 'Sahara', *Betula* (branches), *Triticum aestivum*


**花器:** 中国産陶器
**花材:** バラ"サハラ"、白樺(枝)、コムギ属-aestivum

**VASE:** Chinesische Keramik
**MATERIAL:** *Corylus avellana, Papaver nudicaule*


**VASE:** Chinese pottery
**MATERIAL:** *Corylus avellana, Papaver nudicaule*


**花器:** 中国産陶器
**花材:** ハシバミ属-avellana、ケシ属-nudicaule


**VASE:** Koreanische Keramik in Salbeigrün
**MATERIAL:** *Fallopia japonica* (syn. *Reynoutria*), *Polygonatum multiflorum* (Beeren), *Pinus strobus, Cynara scolymus, Fallopia convolvulus, Papaver somniferum, Hydrangea macrophylla, Tricyrtis hirta, Zea mays*


**VASE:** Korean sageware
**MATERIAL:** *Fallopia japonica* (syn. *Reynoutria*), *Polygonatum multiflorum* (berries), *Pinus strobus, Cynara scolymus, Fallopia convolvulus, Papaver somniferum, Hydrangea macrophylla, Tricyrtis hirta, Zea mays*


**花器:** 韓国産陶器、サルビアグリーン色
**花材:** イタドリ属-japonica、ユリ科-multiflorum(実)、松属-strobus、チョウセンアザミ属-scolymus、タデ科-convolvulus、ケシ属-somniferum、アジサイ属-macrophylla、ホトトギス属-hirta、トウモロコシ属-mays

VASE: Chinesische Keramik mit Perlmutt-Glasur
MATERIAL: *Lunaria annua, Heracleum mantegazzianum,*
*Phalaenopsis, Hordeum jubatum,* Reispapier

VASE: Chinese pottery with mother-of-pearl glaze
MATERIAL: *Lunaria annua, Heracleum mantegazzianum,*
*Phalaenopsis, Hordeum jubatum,* rice paper

花器：中国産陶器、真珠層上薬塗り
花材：アブラナ科-annua、セリ科-mantegazzianum、
ファレノプシス、オオムギ属-jubatum、ライスペーパー

VASE: Zeitgenössische Keramik von Karin Utta Altena/Deutschland
MATERIAL: *Lathyrus odoratus, Anthriscus sylvestris* (Blätter),
*Papaver orientale* (Kapseln), *Briza media, Limonium latifolium,*
*Convolvulus arvensis, Ceropegia woodii*


VASE: contemporary ceramics by Karin Utta Altena/Germany
MATERIAL: *Lathyrus odoratus, Anthriscus sylvestris* (leaves),
*Papaver orientale* (seeds), *Briza media, Limonium latifolium,*
*Convolvulus arvensis, Ceropegia woodii*


花器: 現代陶器-カーリン・ウッタ・アルテナ/ドイツ
花材: マメ科-odoratus、セリ科-sylvestris(葉)、ケシ属-orientale(嚢)、
小判草属-media、イソマツ属-latifolium、昼顔属-arvensis、
カガイモ科woodii

VASE: Zeitgenössische Keramik von Wataru Nakano/Japan
MATERIAL: *Rosa* 'Superstar'
KONSTRUKTION: *Lupinus* (Samen), *Fallopia convolvulus*,
*Rosa* (Stacheln und Stiele), *Aronia melanocarpa*


VASE: contemporary ceramics by Wataru Nakano/Japan
MATERIAL: *Rosa* 'Superstar'
CONSTRUCTION: *Lupinus* (seeds), *Fallopia convolvulus*,
*Rosa* (thorns and stems), *Aronia melanocarpa*


花器: 現代陶器-中野 亘/日本
花材: バラ "スーパースター"
構成: ルピナス(種)、タデ科-convolvulus、バラ(棘、茎)、バラ科-melanocarpa

VASEN: Draht
MATERIAL: *Zantedeschia rehmannii, Dasylirion*


VASES: wire
MATERIAL: *Zantedeschia rehmannii, Dasylirion*


花器: ワイヤー
花材: サトイモ科-rehmannii、リュウゼツラン

FORMEN:  Draht und Bambus
MATERIAL:  *Fritillaria persica, Phormium tenax, Syringa
vulgaris, Iris germanica, Gladiolus,* farblich passende
Trockenmaterialien


FORMS:  wire and bamboo
MATERIAL:  *Fritillaria persica, Phormium tenax, Syringa vulgaris,
Iris germanica, Gladiolus,* dried materials in matching colours


花器: ワイヤー、竹
花材: バイモ属-persica、ユリ科-tenax、モクセイ科-vulgaris、アヤメ属-germanica、
グラジオラス、作品に相応しい色のドライフラワー

ALTE FORMEN NEU ENTDECKT

REDISCOVERING EXISTING FORMS

フォームの再発見

MATERIAL:  gebleichte Dornenzweige, *Rosa* (verschiedene Sorten)


MATERIAL:  bleached thorn branches, *Rosa* (various kinds)


花材: 漂白済棘付枝、バラ(多種)




STRAUSSHALTER:  Original Viktorianischer Straußhalter,
Privatsammlung Jim Moretz/USA
MATERIAL:  *Camellia japonica* (Blüten und Blätter)


BOUQUET HOLDER:  original Victorian bouquet holder,
private collection Jim Moretz/USA
MATERIAL:  *Camellia japonica* (flowers and leaves)


ブーケホルダー: オリジナルヴィクトリア風ブーケホルダー、
ジム・モレッツ/アメリカ 所有
花材: 椿属-japonica(花・葉)

STRAUSSHALTER: Original Viktorianischer Straußhalter,
Privatsammlung Jim Moretz/USA
MATERIAL: *Rosa polyantha*, gebleichte Dornenzweige, Perlen


BOUQUET HOLDER: original Victorian bouquet holder,
private collection Jim Moretz/USA
MATERIAL: *Rosa polyantha*, bleached brambles, beads


ブーケホルダー: オリジナルヴィクトリア風ブーケホルダー、
ジム・モレッツ/アメリカ 所有
花材: バラ科-polyantha、漂白済み棘付枝、真珠

STRAUSSHALTER: Original Viktorianischer Straußhalter,
Privatsammlung Jim Moretz/USA
MATERIAL: *Viola odorata, Salix alba, Jasminum polyanthum*

BOUQUET HOLDER: original Victorian bouquet holder,
private collection Jim Moretz/USA
MATERIAL: *Viola odorata, Salix alba, Jasminum polyanthum*

ブーケホルダー: オリジナルヴィクトリア風ブーケホルダー、
ジム・モレッツ/アメリカ 所有
花材: スミレ属-odorata、柳属-alba、モクセイ科-polyanthum

VASENFORM: *Betula* (Zweigstücke)
MATERIAL: *Fritillaria persica*

VASE FORM: *Betula* (sticks)
MATERIAL: *Fritillaria persica*

器型：白樺(枝)
花材：バイモ属-persica


VASENFORM: *Olea europaea* (Zweigstücke)
MATERIAL: *Celosia argentea* var. *cristata*

VASE FORM: *Olea europaea* (sticks)
MATERIAL: *Celosia argentea* var. *cristata*

器型：オリーブ-europea(枝)
花材：ケイトウ属-argentea


VASENFORM: *Euonymus alatus* (Zweigstücke)
MATERIAL: *Cynara scolymus*

VASE FORM: *Euonymus alatus* (sticks)
MATERIAL: *Cynara scolymus*

器型：錦木-alatus(枝)
花材：チョウセンアザミ属-scolymus

**MATERIAL:** *Limonium sinuatum, Limonium latifolium, Acacia dealbata, Genista monosperma, Schinus molle, Skimmia japonica, Gypsophila paniculata, Chamelaucium uncinatum*

**MATERIAL:** *Limonium sinuatum, Limonium latifolium, Acacia dealbata, Genista monosperma, Schinus molle, Skimmia japonica, Gypsophila paniculata, Chamelaucium uncinatum*

花材：イソマツ属-sinuatum、イソマツ属-latifolium、アカシア-dealbata、ヒトツバエニシダ属-monosperma、コショウボク属-molle、ミヤマシキミ属-japonica、かすみ草属-paniculata、ワックスフラワー属-uncinatum

**MATERIAL:** *Pinus nigra* (Nadeln), *Symphoricarpos albus* (Beeren)

**MATERIAL:** *Pinus nigra* (needles), *Symphoricarpos albus* (berries)

花材：松属-nigra(葉)、スイカズラ科-albus(実)

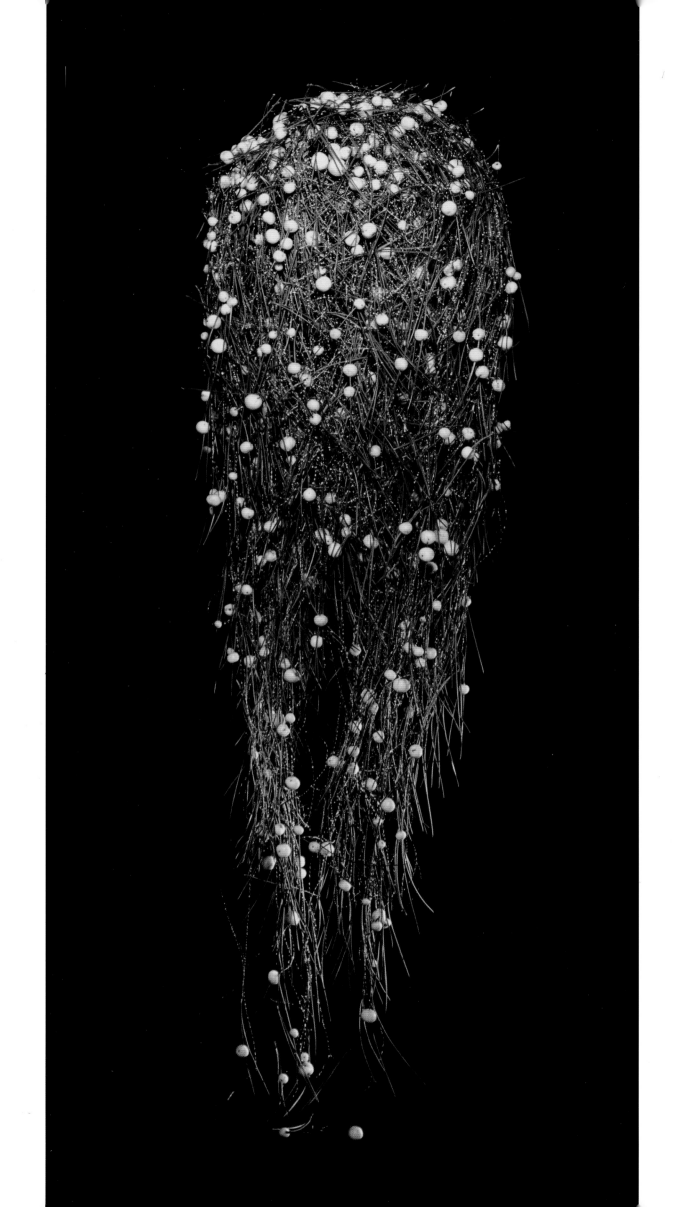

MATERIAL: *Convallaria majalis, Agave sisalana* (= Sisalfaser)

MATERIAL: *Convallaria majalis, Agave sisalana* (= sisal fibers)

花材：鈴蘭属-majalis、リュウゼツラン属-sisalana(=シサル麻)

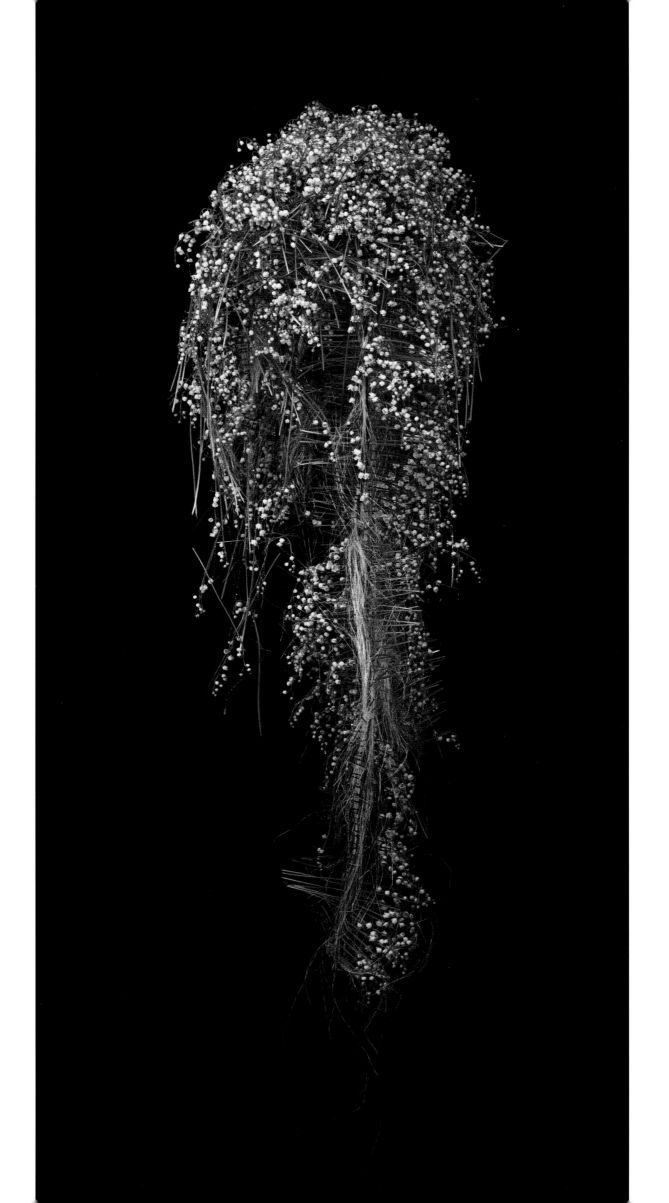

MATERIAL: verschiedene Zweige, *Prunus* (Blüten)

MATERIAL: assortment of twigs, *Prunus* (blossoms)

花材：枝多種、桜(花弁)

KERZE: Altarkerze
MATERIAL:  *Galanthus nivalis*, *Pinus sylvestris* (Zapfen), *Lunaria annua*, *Calocephalus brownii* (trocken), Weihnachtsschmuck

CANDLE:  altar candle
MATERIAL:  *Galanthus nivalis*, *Pinus sylvestris* (cones), *Lunaria annua*, *Calocephalus brownii* (dried), Christmas ornaments

蠟燭: 祭壇用蠟燭
花材: マツユキソウ属-nivalis、松属-sylvestris(毬)、アブラナ科-annua、キク科-brownii(ドライ)、クリスマス飾り

**KRÄNZE:** Draht
**MATERIAL:** *Rosa* 'Piano', *Aronia melanocarpa*


**WREATHS:** wire
**MATERIAL:** *Rosa* 'Piano', *Aronia melanocarpa*


リース: ワイヤー
花材: バラ "ピアノ"、バラ科-melanocarpa




**GEFÄSSE:** Wachs und pflanzliche Trockenmaterialien
**MATERIAL:** *Crocus, Pinus sylvestris*


**CONTAINERS:** wax and dried botanicals
**MATERIAL:** *Crocus, Pinus sylvestris*


花器: 蝋、植物性乾燥資材
花材: クロッカス、松属-sylvestris

SCHALEN: Draht, japanisches Reispapier
MATERIAL: 1. *Malus* (Zweigstücke), 2. *Lavandula* (Blüten),
3. *Pinus* (Nadeln), 4. *Rosa* (Hagebutten), 5. *Heracleum*
(Samen), 6. *Avena* (Stiele), 7. *Schinus* (Beeren), 8. *Illicium
anisatum* (= Sternanis), 9. *Syzygium aromaticum*
(= Gewürznelken)


DISHES: wire, Japanese rice paper
MATERIAL: 1. *Malus* (twigs), 2. *Lavandula* (blossoms), 3. *Pinus*
(needles), 4. *Rosa* (hips), 5. *Heracleum* (seeds), 6. *Avena*
(stems), 7. *Schinus* (berries), 8. *Illicium anisatum* (= star anise),
9. *Syzygium aromaticum* (= cloves)

花器: ワイヤー、和製ライスペーパー
花材: 1.林檎(枝部)、2.ラベンダー(花)、3.松(針)、4.バラ(野茨の実)、5.セリ(種)、
6.バショウ(茎)、7.胡椒(実)、8.シキミ属-anisatum(=ダイウイキョウ)
9.、フトモモ属-aromaticum(=丁子)

MATERIAL: *Tetraria thermalis* (= „Mikado-Stäbe"), *Eremurus robustus, Lunaria annua, Zantedeschia rehmannii, Phalaenopsis, Forsythia* × *intermedia*

MATERIAL: *Tetraria thermalis* (= "Mikado sticks"), *Eremurus robustus, Lunaria annua, Zantedeschia rehmannii, Phalaenopsis, Forsythia* × *intermedia*

花材：パンリード、エルムレス-robustus、アブラナ科-annua、サトイモ科-rehmannii、ファレノプシス、連翹属-× intermedia

KORBFORM: verschiedene Drähte
MATERIAL: *Convallaria majalis, Helleborus niger,*
*Lunaria annua, Nerine bowdenii, Maireana sedifolia* (= Kochia)


BASKET FORM: assortment of wires
MATERIAL: *Convallaria majalis, Helleborus niger,*
*Lunaria annua, Nerine bowdenii, Maireana sedifolia* (= Kochia)


籠型: 多種ワイヤー
花材: 鈴蘭属-majalis、クリスマスローズ属-niger、アブラナ科-annua、
ヒガンバナ科-bowdenii、コキア

KORBBODEN: Wachs
MATERIAL: *Ornithogalum arabicum, Agave sisalana*
(= Sisalfaser), *Typha latifolia*


BASKET BASE: wax
MATERIAL: *Ornithogalum arabicum, Agave sisalana*
(= sisal fibers), *Typha latifolia*


土台：蝋
花材：オーニソガラムarabicum、リュウゼツラン科-sisalana(=シサル麻)、
ガマ属-latifolia

**KORBFORM:** Draht
**MATERIAL:** *Strelitzia nicolai, Allium cepa, Hydrangea macrophylla, Agave americana, Prunus spinosa*


**BASKET FORM:** wire
**MATERIAL:** *Strelitzia nicolai, Allium cepa, Hydrangea macrophylla, Agave americana, Prunus spinosa*


**籠型:** ワイヤー
**花材:** ストレチア-nicolai、アリウム-cepa、アジサイ属-macrophylla、リュウゼツラン属-americana、桜-spinosa

**KORBFORM:** Eisen und Treibholzstücke
**MATERIAL:** *Clematis jackmanii*


**BASKET:** metal and pieces of driftwood
**MATERIAL:** *Clematis jackmanii*


**籠型:** 鉄、流木枝
**花材:** クレマチス-jackmanii

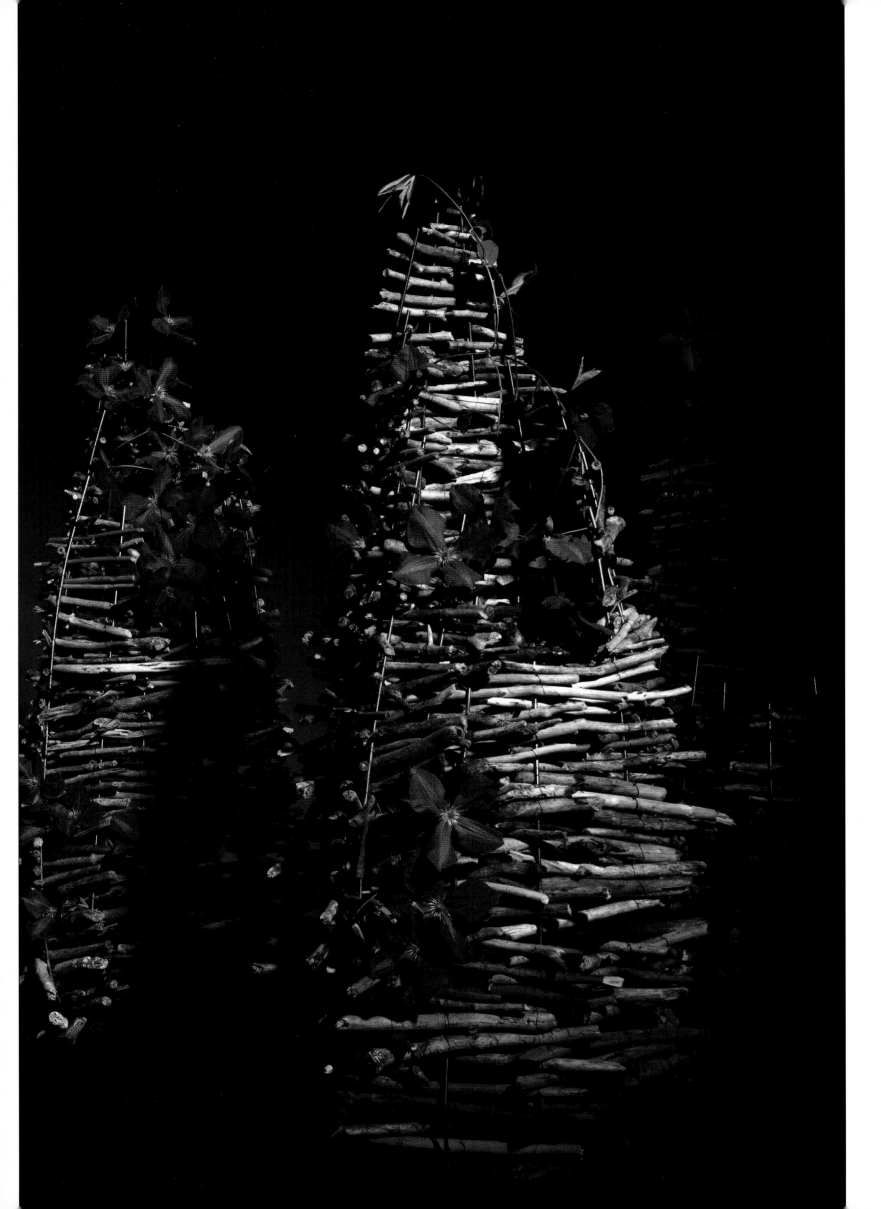

WEST TRIFFT OST

WEST MEETS EAST

西と東の出会い

GEFÄSS: quadratische Glasschale
MATERIAL: *Cornus sericea* 'Flaviramea', *Phormium tenax,*
*Cattleya, Anthurium* 'Midori', *Ornithogalum arabicum,*
*Leucojum vernum*

CONTAINER: square glass dish
MATERIAL: *Cornus sericea* 'Flaviramea', *Phormium tenax,*
*Cattleya, Anthurium* 'Midori', *Ornithogalum arabicum,*
*Leucojum vernum*

花器: 正方形ガラス皿
花材: 水木属-sericea "フラヴィラメア"、ユリ科-tenax、
カトレア、アンスリウム "ミドリ"、オーニソガラム-arabicum、
スノーフレーク属-vernum

GEFÄSS: runde Metallschale
MATERIAL: *Hippeastrum, Ilex aquifolium* (Blätter und Zweige),
*Malus* (Zweige)


CONTAINER: round metal dish
MATERIAL: *Hippeastrum, Ilex aquifolium* (leaves and branches),
*Malus* (branches)

花器: 丸型鉄製皿
花材: アマリリス、モチノキ科-aquifolium(葉・枝)、林檎(枝)


GEFÄSS: Antikes Bronzegefäß („Usubata"), Japan ca. 1800
MATERIAL: *Juniperus communis*, braune Iris


CONTAINER: antique bronze container ("Usubata"),
Japan ca. 1800
MATERIAL: *Juniperus communis*, brown Iris


花器: 銅製古典花器(薄端)、日本 1800年
花材: ヒノキ科-communis、青イリス

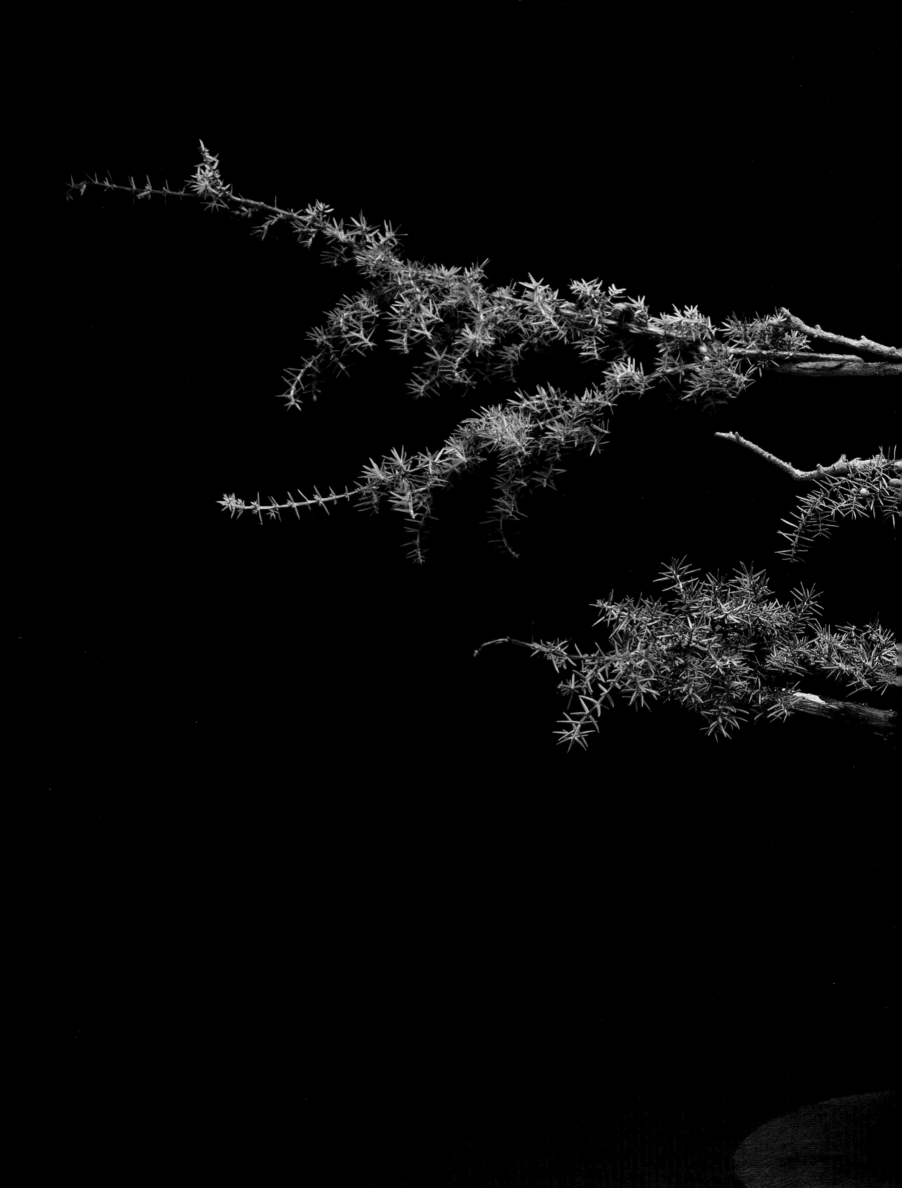

GEFÄSS: klassische japanische Bronzevase
MATERIAL: *Rosa villosa, Malus* (Zweige), *Strelitzia nicolai*


CONTAINER: classic Japanese bronze vase
MATERIAL: *Rosa villosa, Malus* (twigs), *Strelitzia nicolai*


花器: 和製古典銅製花器
花材: バラ-villosa、林檎(枝)、ストレチア-nicolai

GEFÄSS: zeitgenössische Keramik von Kosei Imura/Japan
MATERIAL: *Dendranthema grandiflorum* (syn. *Chrysanthemum*),
*Coccoloba vinifera* (Trockenblätter)

CONTAINER: contemporary pottery by Kosei Imura/Japan
MATERIAL: *Dendranthema grandiflorum* (syn. *Chrysanthemum*),
*Coccoloba vinifera* (dried leaves)

花器: 現代陶器-井村侊生/日本
花材: 菊属-grandiflorum、タデ科-vinifera(ドライの葉)

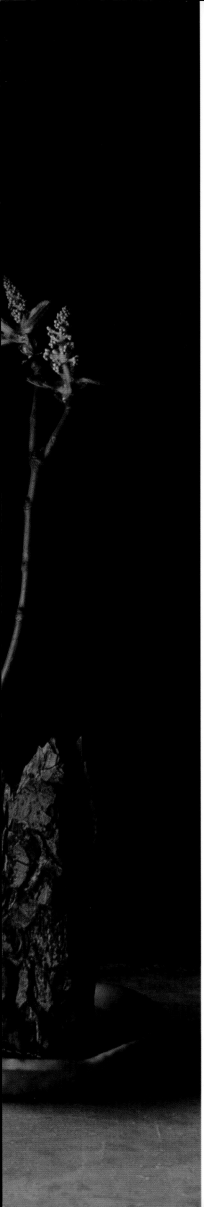

GEFÄSSE: „Shigaraki"-Keramik, Japan
MATERIAL: *Iris germanica, Aesculus hippocastanum* (Zweige)


CONTAINERS: "Shigaraki" pottery, Japan
MATERIAL: *Iris germanica, Aesculus hippocastanum* (branches)


花器: 信楽焼、日本
花材: アヤメ属-germanica、トチノキ属-hippocastanum(枝)


GEFÄSS: Antikes Bronzegefäß („Suiban"), Japan ca. 1800
MATERIAL: *Pinus nigra, Passiflora caerulea, Leucocoryne ixioides*


CONTAINER: antique bronze container ("Suiban"), Japan
ca. 1800
MATERIAL: *Pinus nigra, Passiflora caerulea, Leucocoryne ixioides*


花器: 銅製古典花器(水盤)、日本 1800年代
花材: 松属-nigra、時計草属-caerulea、リューココリネ-ixioides

GEFÄSS: antikes Bronzegefäß („Usubata"), zweiteilig,
Japan ca. 1850
MATERIAL: *Rumex longifolius, Veronica longifolia,*
*Allium oleraceum*


CONTAINER: antique bronze container ("Usubata"), two-piece,
Japan ca. 1850
MATERIAL: *Rumex longifolius, Veronica longifolia,*
*Allium oleraceum*


花器: 銅製古典花器(薄端)、分離型、日本 1850年代
花材: たで科-longifolius、ヴェロニカ-longifolia、アリウム-oleraceum

# INSPIRATION NORWEGEN

# NORWEGIAN INSPIRATION

ノルウェーのインスピレーション

MATERIAL: *Pinus sylvestris*

MATERIAL: *Pinus sylvestris*

花材: 松属-sylvestris

MATERIAL: *Hepatica nobilis*

MATERIAL: *Hepatica nobilis*

花材: キンポウゲ科-nobilis

**MATERIAL:** *Nymphaea* (Stiele), *Calla palustris, Cissus sicyoides, Zantedeschia rehmannii*

**MATERIAL:** *Nymphaea* (stems), *Calla palustris, Cissus sicyoides, Zantedeschia rehmannii*

花材: 睡蓮(茎)、カラー-palustris、ブドウ科-sicyoides、サトイモ科-rehmannii

**MATERIAL:** Norwegische Wildblumen (Juni) wie *Campanula, Trifolium, Rosa,* Gräser, *Anthriscus*

**MATERIAL:** Norwegian wild flowers (collected in June) such as *Campanula, Trifolium, Rosa,* grasses, *Anthriscus*

花材: ノルウェーの野生植物(6月)、カンパニュラ、クローバ、バラ、グラス、チャービル

MATERIAL: *Taraxacum officinale*

MATERIAL: *Taraxacum officinale*

花材: タンポポ属-officinale

**MATERIAL:** Flechtenzweige, *Anemone coronaria*

**MATERIAL:** twisted moss branches, *Anemone coronaria*

花材： 苔付編枝、アネモネ-coronaria

**MATERIAL:** *Betula nigra* (Rinde und Äste), *Forsythia x intermedia*

**MATERIAL:** *Betula nigra* (bark and branches), *Forsythia x intermedia*

花材： カバノキ属-nigra(樹皮、枝)、連翹属-x intermedia

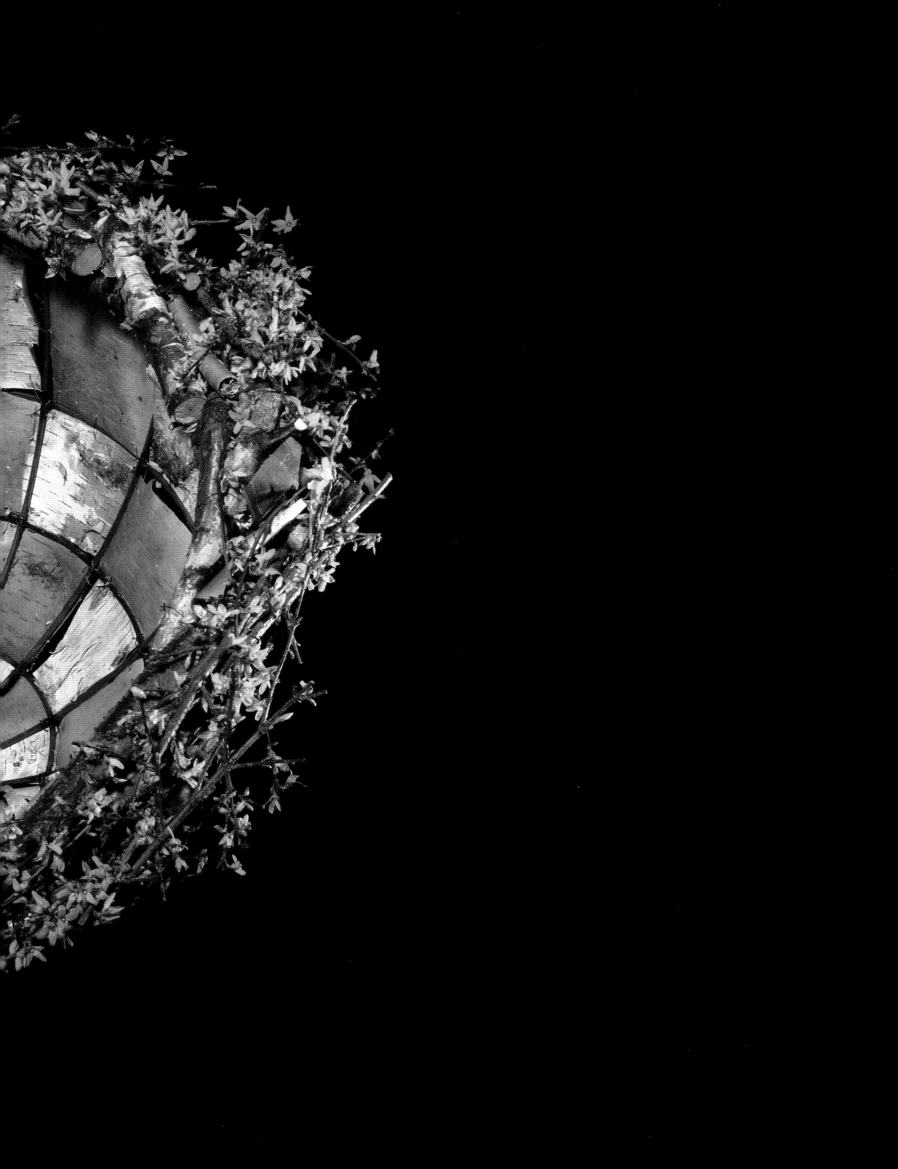

MATERIAL: verschiedene Gräser wie *Holcus lanatus,*
*Hordeum vulgare, Hordeum jubatum, Secale cereale, Dactylis*
*glomerata, Alopecurus pratensis, Bromus benekenii, Tetraria*
*thermalis* („Mikado-Stäbe")

MATERIAL: assortment of grasses such as *Holcus lanatus,*
*Hordeum vulgare, Hordeum jubatum, Secale cereale, Dactylis*
*glomerata, Alopecurus pratensis, Bromus benekenii, Tetraria*
*thermalis* ("Mikado sticks")

花材: グラス多種:シラゲカヤ属-lanatus、オオムギ属-vulgare、オオムギ属-jubatum、
ライムギ属-cereale、カモガヤ属-glomerata、スズメのテッポウ、イネ科-benekenii、
パンリード(ミカドボウ)

MATERIAL: *Tussilago farfara,* trockenes Gras

MATERIAL: *Tussilago farfara,* dried grass

花材: フキタンポポ属-farfara、ドライのグラス

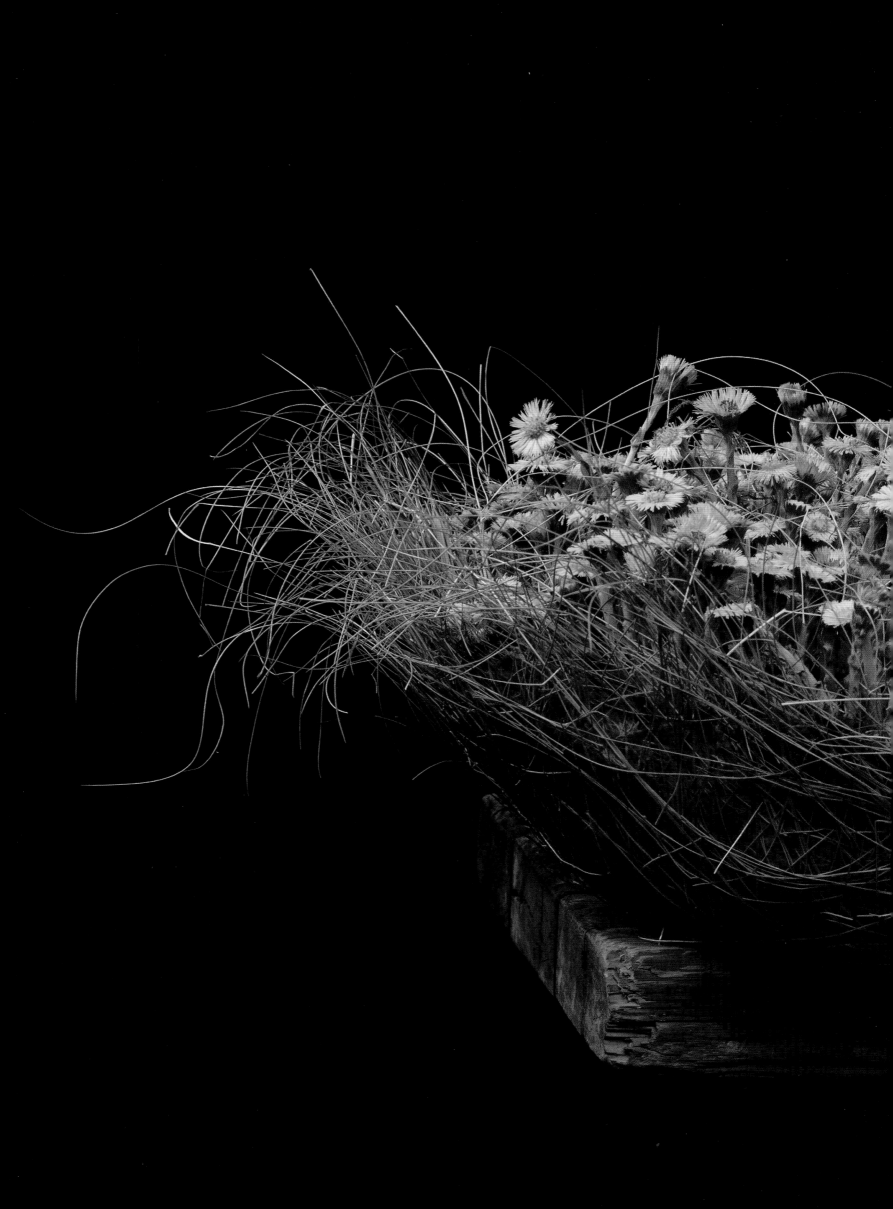

GEFÄSS: Wachs und Schnee
MATERIAL: *Allium neapolitanum*

CONTAINER: wax and snow
MATERIAL: *Allium neapolitanum*

花器: 蝋、雪
花材: アリウム-neapolitanum

# TOR GUNDERSEN

## VITA DES FLORISTEN

Geboren am 2. Juni 1963

**1981** nach 1-jähriger Kunstschule Beginn der Floristausbildung in Volda/Westnorwegen
**1985** Abschlussprüfung Florist

Teilnehmer an mehreren nationalen und internationalen Floristik-Wettbewerben
Gewinner von 20 Medaillen
5x Gewinner der Oslo-Meisterschaft
1x Gewinner des Norwegischen Lehrlingswettbewerbs
**1988** Gewinner der Skandinavischen Meisterschaft
**1994** Gewinner der Norwegen-Meisterschaft
**1995** Gewinner des Europacup

**1989** Teilnehmer für Norwegen beim Interflora Weltcup in Tokio
**1993** Assistent des norwegischen Teilnehmers beim Interflora-Weltcup in Stockholm

Mit Arbeiten vertreten in den Publikationen:
*World Flower Artists I* (Sodo 1989)
*Festival der Sträuße* (FMS 1996)
*Nordic Masters of Flower Arrangement* (Stichting Kunstboek 2001)

Erste Monographie:
*Tor Gundersen* (Sodo 1993)

**1994–1998** freiberuflicher Floraldesigner
**1998** im Dezember Eröffnung eines eigenen Ladens in Oslo
parallel Juryarbeit, Unterrichten und Fach-demonstrationen in über 20 Ländern der Welt

Wichtige Veranstaltungen:
**1996** „Dans på Roser" im „ABC teatret" Oslo/Norwegen
**1996** Ausstellung und Demonstration im Vierjahreszeiten-Hotel Tokio/Japan
**1999** Ausstellung bei Mobach Pottenbakkers in Utrecht/Niederlande
**2000** Ausstellung im Israel Museum in Jerusalem/Israel
**2001** Designer/Formgeber (im 4-köpfigen Floristenteam) für den Blumenschmuck zur Königlichen Hochzeit von Mette-Marit und Kronprinz Haakon in Oslo/Norwegen

Adresse:
Tor Gundersen
Wesselsgate 2
0165 Oslo - Norwegen
Tel. + Fax: +47 – 22 20 08 88
E-Mail: tor.gundersen@interflora.no

## VITA OF THE FLORIST

Born on 2 June 1963

**1981** After one year at art school began working with flowers in Volda/West Norway
**1985** Passed florist examination

Participated in numerous national and international floristry competitions
Winner of 20 medals
5x Oslo champion
1x Winner of the Norwegian competition for students
**1988** Scandinavian champion
**1994** Norwegian champion
**1995** European champion

**1989** Represented Norway at the Interflora World Cup in Tokyo
**1993** Assistant to the Norwegian participant at the Interflora World Cup in Stockholm

Book publications:
*World Flower Artists I* (Sodo 1989)
*Flower Festival* (FMS 1996)
*Nordic Masters of Flower Arrangement* (Stichting Kunstboek 2001)

First monograph:
*Tor Gundersen* (Sodo 1993)

**1994–1998** Freelance floral designer
**1998** Opened own shop in Oslo in December
Parallel jury duty, lectures and professional demonstrations in over 20 countries around the world

Significant events:
**1996** "Dans på Roser" in the "ABC teatret" in Oslo/Norway
**1996** Exhibition and demonstration in the Four Seasons Hotel in Tokyo/Japan
**1999** Exhibition at Mobach Pottenbakkers in Utrecht/Netherlands
**2000** Exhibition in the Israel Museum in Jerusalem/Israel
**2001** Designer (in a team of 4 florists) of the floral decorations for the royal wedding of Mette-Marit and Crown Prince Haakon in Oslo/Norway

Address:
Tor Gundersen
Wesselsgate 2
0165 Oslo
Norway
Tel. + Fax: +47 – 22 20 08 88
E-Mail: tor.gundersen@interflora.no

## フローリスト　略歴

1963　年7月2日生まれ

**1981**　1年間の芸術学校在学の後ヴォルダ/西ノルウェーでのフローリスト研修を始める
**1985**　フローリスト　修了試験

多くの国内・国際競技会への参加
20個のメダル獲得
オスロチャンピオン 5回
ノルウェージュニアチャンピオン 1回
**1988**　スカンジナビアチャンピオン
**1994**　ノルウェーチャンピオン
**1995**　ヨーロッパカップチャンピオン

**1989**　ワールドカップ・東京大会 ノルウェー代表
**1993**　ワールドカップ・ストックホルム大会アシスタント

出版物:
"World Flower Artists I " -
ワールドフラワーアーティスト I (草土出版 1989)
"Festival der Sträuße" (FMS 1996)
"Nordic Masters of Flower Arrangement"
(シュティヒティング クンストブック社2001)

初のモノグラフィー:
"Tor Gundersen"-トゥルー・グンダーセン
(草土出版 1993)

**1994–1998** フリーランスのフラワーデザイナー
**1998.12.**　オスロに花店を開店
同時に世界20以上の国々で審査員、講師、デモストレーターとして活躍

重要な催し:
**1996**　歌劇 "Dans på Roser" ABC劇場
オスロ/ノルウェー
**1996**　展示会＋デモンストレーション
フォーシーズンズホテル 東京/日本
**1999**　展示会　モバッハ ポッテンバッカーズ
ウトレヒト/オランダ
**2000**　展示会　イスラエル美術館
エルサレム/イスラエル
**2001**　メッテ・マーリット、ホーコン皇太子の王室婚礼のデザイナー/造形家(4人のフローリストチーム)
オスロ/ノルウェー

住所:
Tor Gundersen
Wesselsgate 2
0165 Oslo
Norway
Tel.+ Fax: +47 – 22 20 08 88
E-Mail: tor.gundersen@interflora.no

# MONIKA KRATZ

## VITA DER AUTORIN

Die Autorin, Jahrgang 1957, ist nach Germanistik- und Kunstgeschichtsstudium sowie der Ausbildung zur Floristin ab 1990 als Redakteurin und später Chefredakteurin einer deutschen Floristik-Fachzeitschrift tätig gewesen.

Heute arbeitet sie freiberuflich als Fachjournalistin hauptsächlich im Bereich Floristik. Sie veröffentlicht Texte in Fachzeitschriften und special-interest-Zeitschriften im In- und Ausland. Als Moderatorin führt sie durch verschiedene floristische Veranstaltungen wie Symposien, Fachdemonstrationen und Wettbewerbe.

Einen großen Teil nahmen von 1996-2000 die Bühnenshows mit Tor Gundersen vor deutschem Fachpublikum ein, wo sie mit organisierte, moderierte und aus dem Englischen übersetzte.

Mit ihrer eigenen 2001 gegründeten MOKRA-Veranstaltungsreihe „Wege zu Kunst und Kultur" schafft sie ein Forum, wo Menschen der unterschiedlichsten Interessensgebiete sich begegnen. Auch Blumengestaltung gehört dazu.

Monika Kratz hat das floristische Konzept für die Buchreihe „UlmerFloristik" im Verlag Eugen Ulmer, Stuttgart/Deutschland entwickelt. Bisher erschienen sind:
*Blumen im Winter – Floristische Ideen von November bis März* (2000)
*Blumen für den Tisch – Dekorative Ideen für festliche Tafeln* (2001)
*Floristik mit Rosen – Dekorative Ideen für jedes Ambiente* (2001)
*Blumen für das Grab – Floristische Ideen für das ganze Jahr* (2001)
*Blumen im Frühling – Floristische Ideen mit zarten Blüten* (2002)
*Blumen für die Hochzeit – Floristische Ideen für eine traumhafte Trauung* (2002)

Adresse:
Monika Kratz
Ginsterweg 61
50169 Kerpen
Deutschland
Tel.: +49 – 22 73 – 94 17 71
Fax: +49 – 22 73 – 94 17 72
E-Mail: MoKratz@aol.com

## VITA OF THE AUTHOR

The author was born in 1957. After finishing her studies in German and art history she trained as a florist. She worked from 1990 as editor and then editor-in-chief for a German floristry trade journal.

At present she works as a freelance trade journalist mainly in the floristry business. She publishes texts in trade journals and special-interest magazines in Germany and abroad. As a presenter she leads various kinds of floristic events such as symposiums, professional demonstrations and competitions.

A major part of her time between 1996-2000 was spent organizing, presenting and translating (English into German) stage appearances for Tor Gundersen before German audiences.

With her own MOKRA series of events, entitled "Wege zu Kunst and Kultur" (paths to art and culture), initiated in 2001, Monika Kratz created a forum in which people with various interests can meet up and communicate with one another. And flower arranging is definitely one of these interests.

Monika Kratz developed the floristic concept for the "UlmerFloristik" book series for the Eugen Ulmer publishing house, Stuttgart/Germany. At present books are in print on the following topics:
*Flowers in winter* (2000)
*Table flowers* (2001)
*Floristry with roses* (2001)
*Flowers for the cemetery* (2001)
*Spring flowers* (2002)
*Flowers for weddings* (2002)

Address:
Monika Kratz
Ginsterweg 61
50169 Kerpen
Germany
Tel.: +49 – 2273 – 94 17 71
Fax: +49 – 2273 – 94 17 72
E-Mail: MoKratz@aol.com

## 筆者　略歴

1957　年生まれ、独語独文学科-美術史専攻、フローリスト修行、1990年より編集者、後にドイツフローリスト専門誌の編集長

現在フリーランス、主に花卉分野における専門編集者として活躍。専門誌や国内外の特別誌にテキストを発表。シンポジウム、デモンストレーション、競技会を始めとする様々なフローリストの催しの司会。

1996–2000　年ドイツでの専門家向けのトゥル・グンダーセンのショーにてオーガナイザー、司会者、英語からの通訳士として好感を得る。

2001　年独自にMOKRAイベント企画を設立様々な興味深い分野の人々が出会うフォーラム"芸術、文化への道"(花卉デザインを含む)を成功させる。

モニカ・クラッツはEugen Ulmer社(シュトゥットガルト/ドイツ)における一連の"ウルマーフロリスティック"のコンセプトの発展に携わる。今日までの出版物:
"Blumen im Winter - Floristische Ideen von November bis März" (2000) -冬の花
"Blumen für den Tisch - Dekorative Ideen für festliche Tafeln" (2001) -食卓用の花
"Floristik mit Rosen - Dekorative Ideen für jedes Ambiente" (2001) -バラを用いたフローリストデザイン
"Blumen für das Grab - Floristische Ideen für das ganzen Jahr" (2001) -葬儀用の花
"Blumen im Frühling - Floristische Ideen mit zarten Blüten" (2002) -春の花華奢な花を用いたアイディア
"Blumen für die Hochzeit - Floristische Ideen für eine traumhafte Trauung" (2002) -婚礼用の花夢のような結婚式のアイディア

住所:
Monika Kratz
Ginsterweg 61
50169 Kerpen
Germany
Tel.: +49 – 22 73 – 94 17 71
Fax: +49 – 22 73 – 94 17 72
E-Mail: MoKratz@aol.com

# SVEIN-ERIK TØRAASEN

## VITA DES FOTOGRAFEN

Der Fotograf, der die Werke von Tor Gundersen so fantastisch in Szene gesetzt hat, ist 1960 in Norwegen geboren. Er führt in seiner Heimatstadt Oslo ein Studio für digitale Fotografie.

Das „Blueline Studio AS", so der Name seines Unternehmens, gründete er bereits 1987, nachdem er seine Ausbildung am Brooks Institut für Professionelle Fotografie in Santa Barbara, Kalifornien/USA mit Auszeichnung abgeschlossen hatte (Bachelor's degree).

Heute arbeitet er überwiegend mit Firmenkunden und Werbeagenturen zusammen, hauptsächlich im Bereich Still life/Produktfotografie sowie Architekturfotografie.

Im Laufe einiger Jahre gab es schon verschiedene Projekte, die er gemeinsam mit Tor Gundersen realisiert hat. Für die fotografischen Arbeiten zum vorliegenden Buch verwendete er eine Sinar Leaf Volare Digitalkamera, zumeist mit den Sinaron Digital Linsen 55/4.5 mm und 135/5.6, in Kombination mit einem Macintosh G3. Für die Ausleuchtung verwendete er eine Broncolor Studio-Ausrüstung.

Adresse:
Blueline Studio AS
Svein-Erik Tøraasen
P. O. Box 93 Kjelsås
0411 Oslo
Norwegen
Tel. (Studio): +47 – 22 22 22 66
Tel. (Mobil): +47 – 90 84 97 70
Fax: +47 – 22 71 09 75
E-Mail: s-toer@online.no

## VITA OF THE PHOTOGRAPHER

Our photographer, who has so brilliantly captured Tor Gundersen in his pictures, was born in Norway in 1960. He runs a studio for digital photography in his hometown, Oslo. Svein-Erik Tøraasen founded his company, the "Blueline Studio AS", in 1987, after graduating with honours from the Brooks Institute of Professional Photography in Santa Barbara, California/USA (Bachelor's degree). Today he works mostly with corporate clients and advertising agencies, mainly in the areas of still life/product photography and architecture photography. He has been working together with Tor Gundersen for a number of years on several projects. For the photographic work on this book he used a Sinar Leaf Volare digital camera, for the most part with Sinaron digital lenses 55/4.5 mm and 135/5.6, connected to a Macintosh G3. For lighting he uses Broncolor studio equipment.

Address:
Blueline Studio AS
Svein-Erik Tøraasen
P. O. Box 93 Kjelsås
0411 Oslo
Norway
Tel. (Studio): +47 – 22 22 22 66
Tel. (Mobile): +47 – 90 84 97 70
Fax: +47 – 22 71 09 75
E-Mail: s-toer@online.no

## 写真家　略歴

トゥルー・グンダーセンの作品をファンタスティックに演出した写真家はノルウェー生まれ。故郷のオスロでデジタル写真術のスタジオを経営。

アメリカカリフォルニア州サンタバーバラにあるプロの写真術養成所、Brooks Institut(ブルックス インスティテュート)にて学士号を取得後、1987年 "Blueline Studio AS"(ブルーライン スタジオ)を設立。

現在、多くの会社、広告代理店に従事。主に建築写真のような静物/生産写真術。

数年間にトゥール。グンダーセンと共に様々なプロジェクトを実現。この作品集にはSinar Leaf Volare デジタルカメラを使用。多くは55/4.5 mm、135/5.6 mm SinaronデジタルレンズをマッキントッシュG3と共に使用。照明にはBroncolorシステムを使用。

住所:
Blueline Studio AS
Svein-Erik Tøraasen
P.O. Box 93 Kjelsås
0411 Oslo
Norway
Tel. (スタジオ): +47 – 22 22 22 66
Tel. (携帯): +47 – 90 84 97 70
Fax: +47 – 22 71 09 75
E-Mail: s-toer@online.no

## DANK

Perdis Dankertsen
Guro Fjell
Solveig Haugen Andersen
Kai R. Andersen
Kiko Zimmerman
Monika Kratz

Perdis und ihr Mann Jens – die mich in
die Branche einführten und mich dazu
ermutigten, an Wettkämpfen teilzunehmen.

Guro – die mich Bescheidenheit und
respektvollen Umgang mit dem Material
lehrte, und die mir deutlich machte,
wie begrenzt mein Wissen war.

Solveig und Kai – die mir meinen Weg gezeigt
und mich in die richtige Spur gelenkt haben.

Kiko – die meinen Geist aufrecht hält,
das Beste aus mir herausholt und mir sagt,
wer ich bin.

Monika – die so manche besonderen Augen-
blicke mit mir geteilt hat, botanische Erlebnisse und andere Abenteuer, und die dieses
Buchprojekt auf die Beine gestellt hat.

Meine Mitarbeiter im Geschäft – die es
mir erst möglich machen, dass ich meine
Ideen und Konzepte umsetzen kann.

Mein Dank für besondere Unterstützung gilt
Jim Moretz (USA) und Ingvar Strandhs
Blomsterskola (Schweden).

## THANK YOU

Perdis Dankertsen
Guro Fjell
Solveig Haugen Andersen
Kai R. Andersen
Kiko Zimmerman
Monika Kratz

Perdis and her husband Jens – who intro-
duced me to the business and encouraged
me to enter competitions.

Guro – who taught me humbleness and
respect for material and made it clear to me
just how limited my knowledge was.

Solveig and Kai – who showed me the way
and got me on the right track.

Kiko – who kept up my spirit, brought out
the best in me and helped me to discover
who I am.

Monika – who I am grateful to for sharing
moments, botanical experiences and
other adventures, and for making this book
project happen.

The staff in my shop – who make it possible
for me to implement my ideas and concepts.

Special thanks for support go to
Jim Moretz (USA) and Ingvar Strandhs
Blomsterskola (Sweden).

## あとがき-感謝をこめて-

ペアディス・ダンケートセン
ギュロ・フィエル
スルヴァイ・ハウゲン・アンダーソン
カイ・R・アンダーソン
キコ・ジマーマン
モニカ・クラッツ

ペアディスと彼女の夫イェンス-
私をこの道に導き、競技会に参加する事を激励して
くれた方々。

ギュロ-
謙虚さと、材料の扱い方を教えて下さり、私の乏しい
知識を再認識させて下さった方。

スルヴァイ＆カイ-
私の道を開き、正しい方向に指導して下さった方々

キコ-
私の精神を正し、ベストを発揮させ、私が誰であるの
かを言ってくれる人。

モニカ-
数々の冒険、植物的体験を始めとする多くの特別な
一時を共有し、この作品集を企画してくれた人。

店の仲間達-
私のアイディアとコンセプトを最初に可能にしてく
れる人達。

特別支援をして下さったジム(アメリカ)、イングヴ
ァーストランドフラワースクール校(スウェーデン)
に感謝します。

Herzlichen Dank allen, die zu diesem Buch
beigetragen haben!
Tor, der sich damit erneut in eines unserer
„Abenteuer" gewagt hat, für sein hundert-
prozentiges Vertrauen.
Svein-Erik Tøraasen für seine einfühlsame
fotografische Arbeit.
Dr. Nadja Kneissler, Carola Pröpstle,
Ina Vetter und Anke Ruf vom Lektorat sowie
den Übersetzerinnen Janet Brümmer und
Nobuko Yamasaki für ihren begeisterten
Einsatz. Und nicht zuletzt meinem
Lebenspartner O.G.A. für kritisches
Gegenlesen und – unendliche Geduld.

M.K.

My heartfelt thanks to everyone who has
contributed to the creation of this book!
Tor, who was willing to embark on yet
another "adventure" with me, and who gave
me his unwavering confidence.
Svein-Erik Tøraasen for his intuitive photographic work.
Dr. Nadja Kneissler, Carola Pröpstle, Ina
Vetter and Anke Ruf at the editorial office
and also translators Janet Brümmer and
Nobuko Yamasaki for their enthusiastic
efforts. And last but not least, I would like
to thank my partner O.G.A. for his critical
proofreading and – infinite patience.

M.K.

この作品集の出版にあたり貢献して下さったすべて
の方々に心より感謝します！
トゥルー、自身を100パーセント信頼するために、私
たちの新たな"冒険"に敢えて挑んでくれました。
スヴェイン・エリック・トラーセンの心暖まる製作。
ナディア・クナイスラー女史、カロラ・プレプストレ、
編集部のイナ・フェッターとアンケ・ルーフ、そして
翻訳者ジャネット・ブリュマー、山崎信子、彼女たちの
惜しみない協力に。そして、私の人生のパートナー
O.G.A.の批評と限りない忍耐に感謝します。

M.K.

# IMPRINT

**Idea, conception and texts**
Monika Kratz

**English translation**
Janet Brümmer BA, Düsseldorf / Germany
e-mail: janetbruemmer@t-online.de

**Japanese translation**
Nobuko Yamasaki
e-mail: nobuko@mc.kcom.ne.jp

**Photographic credits**
p. 6: Terje Stenstad, Norway
p. 8, 9, 12, 17, 20, 21, 140: Monika Kratz, Germany
p. 13, 14, 142: Kiko Zimmerman, USA
p. 16: Private archives Tor Gundersen, Norway
p. 22: Dana Press / Tor Richardsen, Denmark
p. 23: Bente Hagen, Norway
p. 141: Reiner Haebler, Germany
All other pictures: Svein-Erik Tøraasen, Norway
Drawings p. 10: Tor Gundersen, Norway

**Layout & colour separations**
Graphic Group Van Damme bvba, Oostkamp, Belgium

**Printed by**
Graphic Group Van Damme bvba, Oostkamp, Belgium

**Binding**
Scheerders-Van Kerchove NV, Sint-Niklaas, Belgium

**Published by**
Stichting Kunstboek bvba
Legeweg 165
8020 Oostkamp, Belgium
Tel. + 32 50 46 19 10
Fax: + 32 50 46 19 18
e-mail: stichting_kunstboek@ggvd.com
www.stichtingkunstboek.com

**in co-production with**
Verlag Eugen Ulmer GmbH & Co
Wollgrasweg 41
D-70599 Stuttgart (Hohenheim), Germany

ISBN: 90-5856-066-x
D/2002/6407/9
NUGI: 411